MW00893802

The Art Of Doing Less At Work

By

J. Sharpe

Legal Disclaimer

Introduction

Welcome to "The Art of Doing Less at Work," a humorous (and slightly devious) guide to mastering the fine art of looking busy while doing... not much at all. If you've ever felt like the daily grind is grinding *you* down, this book is here to inject some levity—and a few sly strategies—into your workday. Whether you're deep into *quiet quitting* or just need a break from your inbox, this is the companion you didn't know you needed.

This isn't your typical career advice book filled with buzzwords and motivational platitudes. Instead, it's a hilarious guide packed with strategies for blending in while doing as little as possible. From perfecting the *fake IT crisis* to mastering the *strategic sigh,* you'll learn techniques to outwit your coworkers and bosses while saving your energy for what really matters: literally anything but work. Because let's be honest: some days, the only thing standing between you and your resignation letter is the ability to laugh through the chaos.

So, set your out-of-office reply, grab your spreadsheet of meaningless figures, and let's explore the world of doing less—because why work harder when you can work smarter—or not at all?

1. Master the Art of Walking Briskly While Carrying a Clipboard

Ah, the clipboard: a timeless prop in the grand theater of workplace fakery. This innocuous object, when paired with a determined stride, transforms you into a person of utmost importance. Holding it gives you the aura of someone who's too busy saving the company to answer pesky questions like "What are you working on?" or "Can you help me for a minute?" But here's the real trick—keeping that clipboard empty.

Step 1: Acquire the Perfect Clipboard
Not just any clipboard will do. A shiny new one screams "I'm pretending," while a weathered clipboard says, "This is my job, and I've been at it for years." Bonus points for slapping on an official-looking sticker from an event you "helped run" years ago.

Step 2: Perfect the Stride
You're not sauntering—you're on a mission. Channel the energy of someone who just remembered they left their oven on. Walk quickly enough to avoid interactions but not so fast that you trip over your own shoes. If your coworkers try to stop you, flash them a "not now" hand signal and mutter something vague like, "Quarterly projections wait for no one."

Step 3: The Face of Urgency
Your face is key. You need to strike the perfect balance between mild panic and quiet confidence. Picture someone who just realized they're low on toner right before a

deadline but knows exactly where the backup cartridges are.

Step 4: Avoid Stalling

Never, ever stand still. A stationary clipboard-holder invites questions like, "Hey, can you help with this?" or worse, "What are you working on?" If you must stop, linger near a copy machine, a whiteboard, or a water cooler. These places exude "business vibes."

Step 5: The Script

Prepare a few generic phrases to throw out if anyone dares ask what you're doing. Gems like:

- "Just following up on some action items."
- "You know how it is—always something in the pipeline!"
- "Need to touch base with [insert important-sounding name]."

Advanced Techniques

Once you've mastered the basics, you can elevate your act. For instance, bring a pen and occasionally make mysterious marks on the clipboard. Bonus points for furrowing your brow while nodding slightly, as if solving the company's greatest problem. If you're feeling ambitious, tape a blank spreadsheet onto the clipboard for added legitimacy.

The Ultimate Escape Plan

If your boss catches on and asks for updates, keep your answer simple and peppered with buzzwords. Say something like, "I'm still gathering insights to align with our KPIs," and walk away before they can respond.

By following this method, you'll spend your workdays strutting around with purpose while accomplishing absolutely nothing. Remember, the empty clipboard isn't just a tool—it's a lifestyle. Carry it with pride and let it do all the hard work of looking busy, so you don't have to!

2. Always Look Deeply Concerned When Staring at Your Computer Screen

The art of looking busy often lies in the subtle performance of looking stressed. And what better prop than your trusty computer screen? Staring at it with an expression of deep concern will make you appear so immersed in a critical task that no one will dare interrupt. It's an illusion so convincing that even *you* might forget you're actually watching cat videos on YouTube.

Step 1: Set the Scene
Before you begin your Oscar-worthy performance, arrange your desk for maximum believability. Open a spreadsheet or a complicated chart in one tab and position it so anyone walking by can see it. In another tab, pull up something less... productive, like ranking your favorite snacks or browsing vacation destinations.

Keep an additional tab open with your email inbox. The more unread messages, the better. Bonus points if the subject lines sound intense, like "URGENT: Deadline Approaching" or "Follow-Up Needed ASAP." These will serve as your digital props, silently screaming "I'm swamped!" to anyone within earshot.

Step 2: The Concerned Expression
This is the pièce de résistance. Start with furrowed brows—it's a universal sign of deep thought. Add a slight squint, as if you're analyzing data so complex it would make Einstein cry. Tilt your head just enough to look like you're considering a breakthrough idea but not so much that you look confused.

Optional: Occasionally lean back and sigh. The more audible, the better. A well-timed, "Huh..." will further sell the act.

Step 3: Fake the Body Language
Don't just sit there; commit with your whole body! Rest your chin on your hand for a pensive pose. Tap your keyboard occasionally—randomly, if necessary—but make it sound deliberate. Pro tip: Hit the spacebar repeatedly to create the illusion of typing without risking a typo.

If anyone glances over, click your mouse rapidly, as if toggling between important documents. No one will notice you're toggling between a meme and a recipe for 30-minute lasagna.

Step 4: Diversion Tactics
When a coworker inevitably interrupts you with a question, do *not* break character. Slowly lift your head as if emerging from a mental labyrinth. Say something like, "Sorry, what? I was just figuring out how to integrate these metrics into the new framework." If they press for details, shake your head and say, "It's hard to explain without context."

Advanced Techniques

For the seasoned faker, adding small props can elevate your performance. A stack of unopened files next to your keyboard says, "I'm so busy I haven't even gotten to these yet." Scribble random notes in a journal while staring at the screen, muttering phrases like "Why isn't this syncing?" under your breath.

Prolong the Act

When your boss walks by, switch tabs to something that looks serious but incomprehensible—like a calendar full of overlapping meetings or a spreadsheet with lots of numbers. If they ask how it's going, sigh and say, "Honestly? It's been a *day*." They'll back away slowly, leaving you free to laugh at another meme.

With this technique, you'll master the delicate balance of looking both important and overwhelmed, all while doing absolutely nothing. Because at the end of the day, isn't that what work-life balance is all about?

3. Schedule a Recurring "Meeting" with Yourself Every Day—Call It "Strategic Vision Alignment"

Few things scream "important employee" more than a jam-packed calendar. By scheduling a daily, non-negotiable "meeting" with yourself, you're creating the perfect alibi to avoid any real work. The beauty of this tactic lies in the ambiguity: no one knows what "Strategic Vision Alignment" is, and they'll be too intimidated to ask.

Step 1: Set It Up
Open your calendar and block out an hour every day during peak productivity times. (Pro tip: Late morning or early afternoon is ideal—right when people are likely to ask for help.) Label the meeting something vague but professional. "Strategic Vision Alignment" is a classic, but feel free to mix it up with options like:
- "Workflow Optimization Planning"
- "Core Metric Evaluation"
- "Cross-Departmental Synergy Brainstorm"

If you're feeling particularly cheeky, use acronyms like SVA or CDEB—no one will know what they mean, and that's exactly the point.

Step 2: Make It Look Legit
Set the meeting to "private" so coworkers can't click into it and discover it's just you. Add an alarm so your phone dings at the start—nothing says "important meeting" like a loud reminder. If your office has meeting rooms, book one occasionally to avoid suspicion. Bonus points if it's a room with frosted glass so people see you but can't tell what you're doing.

Step 3: Appear Busy
During your "meeting," stay at your desk or head to the designated room. If you're at your desk, keep your headset on (even if you're just listening to a podcast). Occasionally nod or scribble something on a notepad. If anyone asks what you're working on, mumble something about "actionable deliverables" and go back to staring at your screen.

Step 4: Field Interruptions
Should someone dare to interrupt your sacred meeting time, remain calm but firm. Hold up a finger to signal "just a moment" and whisper, "I'm in the middle of something important." They'll either walk away or feel so awkward they'll leave you alone for the rest of the day.

If they persist, sigh dramatically and say, "This is a delicate time for the strategy pivot we've been discussing." Then immediately excuse yourself with, "I really can't talk right now, but let's follow up."

Step 5: What to Do During the "Meeting"
Now comes the fun part: your meeting is an open hour to do whatever you want. Want to online shop? Go for it. Need a nap? Close your office door and tilt your chair back. Feel like catching up on Netflix? Call it "market research."

Advanced Techniques
For an extra layer of believability, occasionally update colleagues about your "progress." Say things like, "Our strategic alignment is really coming together" or "We're uncovering some exciting insights." Use vague buzzwords, and they'll nod in agreement without a clue.

Bonus Points
Find an equally lazy co-worker and schedule the meeting with them, safe in the knowledge that neither of you will be attending it. Teamwork makes the dream work!

The Perfect Alibi
The genius of this tactic is that no one will challenge you. People respect "meetings," and as long as you keep the

charade alive, your Strategic Vision Alignment will remain a fortress of solitude in the chaotic world of work.

Congratulations, you've turned scheduling software into a tool for glorious procrastination. With your daily "meeting," you'll always look busy while doing less. Who knew corporate buzzwords could be this liberating?

4. Learn to Say, "I'll Circle Back on That," and Then Forget About It Entirely

"I'll circle back on that" is the Swiss Army knife of corporate jargon—a phrase so vague and noncommittal it could mean anything or nothing at all. It's the ultimate escape hatch, letting you deftly sidestep tasks while sounding like you're on top of things. The beauty of this line is its simplicity: it's polite, professional, and a surefire way to move the conversation along without actually committing to anything.

Step 1: Master the Tone
Delivery is everything. When saying, "I'll circle back on that," you need to sound engaged but slightly preoccupied—like you're mentally juggling a dozen high-priority tasks. Use a tone that says, "I hear you, and I care deeply about this... but not enough to act right now."

Pro tip: Add a small nod as you say it, as if mentally bookmarking their request. This visual cue reassures them you're on it (you're not).

Step 2: Deploy at the Right Moment
This phrase is most effective when someone asks you to:
- Take on extra work ("Can you run those reports by EOD?")
- Clarify something you don't understand ("What's our Q2 retention strategy?")
- Participate in a project you'd rather avoid ("Can you join the brainstorming session?")

In these moments, calmly say, "Great point, let me circle back on that," and watch their relief as they believe you'll handle it. You won't.

Step 3: Ensure Forgetfulness
For maximum effectiveness, make no effort to remember the task. If they bring it up again, act surprised: "Oh, I thought we resolved that already! Let me double-check and circle back on that."

Repeat the cycle as needed.

Alternatively, pretend someone else dropped the ball: "I was waiting for feedback from Steve before moving forward. Let me check in with them." (Spoiler: you won't.)

Step 4: Pair It With Buzzwords
To further baffle and appease, sprinkle in phrases like:
- "Let me take that offline for now."
- "I'll align with the team and touch base later."
- "We'll loop back once we've fleshed out the details."

These phrases sound action-oriented but mean absolutely nothing, which is exactly what you want.

Advanced Techniques

For seasoned pros, take "circling back" to the next level by creating a phantom "to-do list." Whenever someone asks for an update, smile and say, "It's on my list!" No one will ask to see the list, and you can confidently maintain that the task is "in progress" forever.

Escape Hatch Backup Plan

If pressed for a deadline, respond with, "I want to make sure I give this the attention it deserves, so let me confirm timelines and get back to you." They'll appreciate your fake thoroughness and move on to someone else.

Warning Signs to Watch For

If someone keeps following up, your cover might be blown. In this case, respond with, "Oh, I was under the impression this was no longer a priority—should we revisit?" This flips the blame back onto them while buying you even more time to do... nothing.

"I'll circle back on that" isn't just a phrase; it's a philosophy of avoidance disguised as professionalism. Used correctly, it can make you look like a team player while leaving you free to relax. So, next time someone asks you to handle something, remember: circling back is your golden ticket to doing less!

5. Volunteer to Organize the Supply Closet—It'll Take Months

Few tasks provide the perfect cover for prolonged idleness like "organizing the supply closet." It's a project that sounds necessary and selfless but can stretch on indefinitely. No one will bother you, and better yet, they'll even thank you for "taking the initiative." Little do they know, you've found the workplace equivalent of disappearing into the Bermuda Triangle.

Step 1: Volunteer with Enthusiasm
When the topic of the supply closet comes up in a meeting—because every workplace has *that* closet—jump in quickly: "I've been meaning to tackle that! It's chaotic in there." You'll immediately earn brownie points for your "can-do" attitude, even though your real motivation is to hide among the pens and Post-it notes.

Optional: Throw in a little self-deprecating humor, like, "I guess my inner Marie Kondo is finally coming out!" This makes your offer seem genuine, not strategic.

Step 2: Scope Out the Chaos
Once you've secured the gig, visit the supply closet and dramatically shake your head. Mutter phrases like, "Wow, this is worse than I thought," or, "How has anyone been finding anything in here?" This reinforces the idea that the task is monumental, justifying your need for excessive time to complete it.

Take photos of the disarray on your phone—bonus points if you dramatically email them to your boss with the subject line, "Project Update: The Before."

Step 3: Plan an Overly Complicated System
Announce that you're devising a "streamlined inventory system" that will revolutionize how the office uses supplies. Draft a color-coded spreadsheet, complete with supply

categories, subcategories, and hypothetical reorder points. You'll never actually use it, but it looks impressive and buys you weeks of prep time.

Mention needing special bins or dividers "to do it right." This opens the door for multiple trips to office supply stores, which can consume entire afternoons.

Step 4: Work Slowly and Methodically
Begin the project, but pace yourself. Move items from one shelf to another, only to move them back the next day. Shuffle papers around while sighing dramatically. Spend hours "debating" whether the highlighters should be organized by color or brand. This makes it look like you're invested in the details, when really, you're just biding your time.

Step 5: Regular Status Updates
Keep your coworkers informed of your "progress." Share updates like:
- "I've sorted out 40% of the folders, but I'm still refining the system."
- "I just realized we're out of label tape, so I need to pause until we get more."
- "Did you know we have six different kinds of binder clips? Crazy, right?"

These updates make it seem like you're working tirelessly, even though you've spent most of the day scrolling on your phone.

Step 6: Prolong the Process
Whenever someone asks when you'll be done, say, "I don't want to rush this—I really want it to last this time." People

respect thoroughness, even if it's just about where the Sharpies go.

Advanced Techniques
To drag things out even longer, claim you've identified inefficiencies in how supplies are ordered and offer to "research better systems." This gives you carte blanche to disappear into spreadsheets and online shopping carts indefinitely.

By the time you "finish" the project (or get reassigned), the supply closet may look marginally better, but your real victory is the hours, days, or even months of peace and quiet you gained in the process. Who knew chaos could be so productive—at least for you?

6. Always Find Out the Office Gossip and Use "Did You Hear About..." to Dodge Uncomfortable Questions

Office gossip isn't just entertainment—it's a survival tool. By staying plugged into the grapevine, you can shift the focus from yourself at a moment's notice. When someone asks you an uncomfortable question, simply pivot with the ultimate distraction: "Did you hear about...?" This not only deflects attention but also reinforces your role as the office's unofficial news source.

Step 1: Cultivate Your Gossip Network
Make it your mission to know everything that's going on in the office. Everyone's business is now your business. Chat with the usual gossip hubs:

- The breakroom coffee crew.
- The lunch group that always whispers conspiratorially.
- The IT team (they know *everything*).

Ask open-ended questions like, "What's new around here?" or "Anything interesting happening lately?" without looking too obvious.

Step 2: Keep a Gossip Rolodex
Mentally catalog every piece of juicy gossip, from "Who's dating who?" to "Who totally bombed that presentation?" The more stories you know, the better equipped you'll be to pivot away from awkward topics later.

Pro tip: Stay neutral and nonjudgmental when hearing gossip. This ensures people keep spilling the tea to you.

Step 3: Deploy the Pivot
When someone asks you an uncomfortable question—like why you're behind on a task or whether you actually attended that meeting—immediately shift the focus with:
- "Oh, speaking of which, did you hear about [random coworker] and [dramatic situation]?"
- "Wait, this reminds me—did you hear what happened in [another department]?"
- "Not to change the subject, but did you hear about the [unexpected office event]?"

Make the gossip sound urgent or surprising to capture their full attention.

Step 4: Lean Into the Gossip
Once the conversation shifts, keep it going with follow-up questions:
- "Can you believe they actually did that?"
- "What do you think will happen next?"
- "I wonder how [boss/coworker] is going to handle it."

Encourage speculation and opinions to prolong the discussion, ensuring the original question is forgotten.

Step 5: Use Gossip as a Shield
To further solidify your role as the office's go-to gossip resource, casually share harmless tidbits even when you're not under pressure. This keeps coworkers coming to you for updates instead of scrutinizing your work.

Examples:
- "Did you hear they're thinking about rearranging the seating chart again?"
- "Rumor has it [new hire] is already planning to leave."
- "I heard [coworker] might be up for that promotion—interesting, right?"

The more you share, the less people will focus on you.

Advanced Techniques
For master-level gossip-pivoters:
- If the person you're pivoting with doesn't know the gossip, say, "Oh, I probably shouldn't say too much—just keep an ear out." This keeps them intrigued while shifting the focus further away from you.

- Pretend to "remember" additional details mid-conversation to keep the story going.
- Drop hints about "something big" coming soon: "Oh, I can't say yet, but you'll know when you see it."

The Backup Plan
If someone tries to redirect the conversation back to you, counter with:
- "Sorry, I got sidetracked! What were we talking about?" (then pivot again).
- "Oh, I'll handle that later—I was just so shocked about [gossip topic]."
- "Let's circle back to that, but seriously, can you believe [gossip]?"

These moves ensure you remain the master of distraction.

By staying in the loop with office gossip and expertly using "Did you hear about...?" to redirect conversations, you've turned workplace drama into a tactical advantage. You're not just avoiding scrutiny—you're the conductor of the office symphony of intrigue. Bravo, gossip guru!

7. Ask a Coworker for "Five Minutes to Chat" Thirty Minutes Before Lunch

Timing is everything in the game of avoiding work, and there's no better time to corner a coworker than right before lunch. It's the golden hour when people are too hungry to focus and too polite to turn you down. By initiating a "quick chat," you've successfully disrupted their flow *and* bought yourself time to do less—all while looking like a team player.

Step 1: Choose the Perfect Target
Identify a coworker who:
1. Looks mildly stressed but not overwhelmed.
2. Is known for their politeness or desire to help.
3. Has a tendency to ramble when answering questions.

Bonus points if this coworker loves brainstorming sessions. You're about to waste time together in the most productive-looking way possible.

Step 2: The Approach
Thirty minutes before lunch, casually stroll over to your target's desk or ping them on Slack. Use a friendly but slightly urgent tone and say, "Hey, do you have five minutes? I just need to pick your brain about something." The phrase "pick your brain" is key—it flatters them into thinking you value their expertise.

Step 3: The "Discussion"
Once they agree (because who says no to "just five minutes"?), start with something broad and nebulous. For example:
- "I've been thinking about how we could streamline [insert vague process]. What do you think?"
- "I'm trying to wrap my head around this upcoming project—any advice?"
- "How do you usually handle [insert hypothetical situation]?"

These open-ended questions encourage long-winded answers. Nod thoughtfully, interject with the occasional "Interesting, tell me more," and let them do most of the talking.

Step 4: Keep an Eye on the Clock

As the conversation drifts on until lunchtime, subtly glance at the clock and say, "Wow, I didn't realize it was already noon! I should grab lunch." This achieves two things:

1. You've successfully stalled until lunchtime without actually working.
2. You've set the stage to end the conversation quickly once it's your lunch break.

Step 5: The Lunch Break Extension

If you've played your cards right, your coworker will suggest continuing the discussion after lunch. Congratulations, you've now secured a longer break under the guise of collaboration!

After lunch, steer the conversation toward non-work topics like weekend plans, favorite TV shows, or whether pineapple belongs on pizza. The longer you keep it lighthearted, the less likely anyone will remember what the original "five-minute chat" was about.

Advanced Techniques

For added flair, bring a notepad to the chat and jot down meaningless notes like "synergy" or "action items." This makes it look like you're deeply engaged, even if you're doodling cats in the margins. If someone asks later what you discussed, reply with something vague but impressive, like, "We explored some innovative approaches to team efficiency. Very promising!"

Warning Signs
If your coworker starts wrapping up the conversation too soon, pivot by asking, "Oh, and one more thing..." before launching into a fresh tangent. This tactic can keep you chatting indefinitely.

By using this strategy, you'll turn a simple question into a pre-lunch productivity killer—and maybe even score an extra-long lunch break. It's a win-win situation (for you, anyway). So, next time you're looking to dodge a task, remember: "five minutes" is just code for "until lunch!"

8. Pretend You Didn't See That Email—For a Week

Email is both a blessing and a curse. It's a convenient way to communicate, but it's also the perfect excuse for delay. "Oh, I must have missed that email" is a classic move in the art of doing less at work. By pretending you didn't see it—or claiming it got buried in your inbox—you can effortlessly buy yourself extra time while appearing innocent.

Step 1: Set the Stage
To make this strategy work, your inbox needs to look chaotic. The more unread messages, the better. This gives you plausible deniability when someone inevitably asks why you haven't responded. If your inbox is too organized, deliberately ignore a few emails to create a backlog.

Bonus tip: Turn off read receipts. You don't want anyone knowing when you've actually opened an email.

Step 2: The "Accidental Overlook"
When you receive an email that involves actual work, don't panic. Instead, let it sit. Resist the urge to even glance at it; this makes it easier to later claim you didn't see it. If it's marked as "urgent," chuckle softly to yourself—because urgency is their problem, not yours.

Step 3: The Grace Period
The key is timing. Let the email marinate for about a week. During this period, act completely oblivious. Participate in team meetings, Slack chats, or hallway conversations as if that email never existed. If someone brings it up, furrow your brow and say, "Oh, was that in an email? I must have missed it—I've been swamped."

Step 4: The Grand Rediscovery
After the appropriate amount of time, suddenly "discover" the email. Respond with faux sincerity:
- "Oh my goodness, I just saw this—I'm so sorry for the delay!"
- "Not sure how this slipped past me, thanks for following up!"
- "This must've gotten buried, but I'm on it now!"

Your feigned enthusiasm for addressing the issue will make you look like a team player, despite the fact that you've been actively ignoring it.

Step 5: Delay Further
Now that you've acknowledged the email, you're not off the hook—but don't worry, there's still room to stall. Respond with a question or request for clarification. Examples include:
- "Could you remind me of the context here?"

- "Do we have the latest data for this?"
- "Let me loop in [insert another coworker] for their input."

These follow-ups ensure the ball is back in their court, not yours.

Advanced Techniques
For true masters of email evasion, blame technology. Claim the email went to your spam folder or got lost in the shuffle during a server glitch. Say things like, "My inbox has been acting up lately—I need to contact IT about it." This not only shifts the blame but also makes you look like the victim of modern technology's shortcomings.

Bonus Points
If you can stall long enough, someone else will inevitably resolve the issue in the email, sparing you from having to lift a finger to address it.

The Backup Plan
If the sender grows impatient, apologize profusely and promise to prioritize their request. Then wait another day or two before actually doing anything. By the time you respond, they'll just be grateful you finally got around to it and will have lower expectations in future.

By pretending you didn't see that email, you've turned procrastination into an art form. You'll maintain plausible deniability, avoid immediate work, and come out looking like the hero who "finally" got things done. Who knew email could be this fun?

9. Spend the First 30 Minutes of the Day Cleaning Coffee Mugs That Were Already Clean

Starting your day with a clean mug is a non-negotiable workplace ritual—or at least, that's the excuse you'll use to delay doing anything productive. The beauty of this strategy lies in its passive-aggressive helpfulness: by "cleaning" mugs that are already spotless, you appear to be the office hero while avoiding any real work. Plus, no one can get mad at someone who's "just trying to help."

Step 1: The Setup
As soon as you walk into the office, head to the break room or communal kitchen. Make a big show of inspecting the mugs in the drying rack. Pick one up, hold it to the light, and frown slightly. Turn it over in your hands like you're analyzing a priceless artifact. Mutter something like, "Wow, these don't feel very clean. Did someone skip the soap again?" This is your golden ticket to wasting time while looking like a selfless team player.

Step 2: Announce Your Plan
Loudly declare, "I'll just give these a quick wash—better safe than sorry, right?" Smile in a way that suggests you're doing this for the good of the team, not because you're avoiding spreadsheets. If anyone protests with "I think they're clean," shake your head solemnly and say, "Trust me, it's easier to just do it now than have someone get sick later."

Step 3: The Prolonged Cleaning Ritual

Now, the real work begins—well, not *real* work. Wash each mug slowly and methodically, scrubbing invisible spots and rinsing for what feels like an eternity. Occasionally squint at a random mug and mutter, "Is that a smudge? Or a shadow?" Proceed to wash it again, just in case.

If someone walks in, smile warmly and say, "Just tidying up—these weren't up to snuff!" They'll either nod in approval or slink away, not wanting to argue with your impeccable hygiene standards.

Step 4: The Over-the-Top Drying Process

After washing, spend extra time drying the mugs. Use paper towels and carefully buff each one until it "gleams." Hold one up like Simba in *The Lion King* and declare, "There we go—*that's* how a clean mug should look!"

Optional: Reorganize the mugs in the cabinet while loudly proclaiming, "This will make it easier for everyone to find their favorite mug." This move adds another 10 minutes to your delay tactic while making you look even more helpful.

Step 5: The Subtle Guilt Trip

When a coworker inevitably grabs a mug from your freshly cleaned batch, smile and say, "Oh, you're welcome! Just wanted to make sure everything was hygienic for you." They'll feel too guilty to question whether the mugs were dirty in the first place.

Advanced Techniques

For the pros, incorporate some extra drama:

- Find a "stain" on a mug (it's just a shadow) and gasp audibly.

- Invent a story about someone getting a cold sore from a dirty mug at your *last* job.
- Suggest starting a "clean mug protocol," which involves daily inspections (led by you, of course).

The Aftermath
By the time you're finished, 30 minutes (or more) will have passed, and you'll have successfully dodged morning meetings or early tasks. The best part? Everyone thinks you're a saint for tackling the "dirty" mugs, and no one will dare criticize you for being "too helpful."

Congratulations, you've turned a harmless stack of clean mugs into a morning-long productivity shield. After all, who can fault you for prioritizing the team's health over getting to work on time?

10. Use the Phrase, "That's Above My Pay Grade," Liberally

Few phrases in the workplace shut down conversations faster than, "That's above my pay grade." It's the perfect way to dodge responsibility without sounding lazy—you're simply acknowledging the limits of your role! This simple yet powerful statement lets you pass the buck while maintaining an air of humility.

Step 1: Deploy With Precision
The trick to mastering this move is knowing when to use it. Key opportunities include:
- When someone tries to delegate a task that's clearly boring or tedious.

- When you're asked a question you don't feel like answering.
- When someone suggests you take initiative on a "stretch project."

For example, if a coworker asks, "Can you take the lead on this client pitch?" respond with, "That sounds like something more suited for management. Definitely above my pay grade!" You'll dodge the responsibility, and they'll likely agree without further questioning.

Step 2: Perfect the Delivery
Your tone should be equal parts respectful and self-effacing. Pair the phrase with a small shrug or an apologetic smile. This makes it clear you're not refusing out of laziness but rather out of a deep respect for organizational hierarchy.

Bonus points if you throw in a chuckle, as if to say, "Ah, the joys of being a mere mortal in this corporate machine."

Step 3: Redirect Responsibility
Whenever possible, follow up your "above my pay grade" declaration with a suggestion that shifts the task to someone else. Examples include:
- "That sounds like a decision for the department head."
- "We should definitely loop in [insert boss's name] on this."
- "I think this aligns more with [coworker's name]'s expertise."

This way, you're not just avoiding the work—you're actively steering it toward someone else. A truly advanced form of workplace ninja skills!

Step 4: Use Buzzwords for Extra Flair

If you want to sound even more convincing, add some corporate jargon to your response. For instance:

- "That's above my pay grade, but I'm happy to support in an auxiliary capacity."
- "Sounds like something that requires executive oversight. Let's escalate this."
- "I think this falls under strategic alignment, so we should loop in leadership."

People will be so distracted by your professional vocabulary that they'll forget you just weaseled out of a task.

Step 5: Deflect and Disappear

If someone insists you take on the task despite your polite protest, deflect further by asking for unnecessary clarification:

- "Can you outline the exact deliverables you're looking for?"
- "Would it be possible to get some guidance from leadership first?"

By the time they've provided answers, the moment of urgency will have passed, and they'll likely give the task to someone else.

Advanced Techniques

For true masters of the phrase, use it to avoid accountability altogether. If a project goes sideways and someone asks for an explanation, simply say, "That decision was above my pay grade." This subtly implies someone higher up is to blame, while you remain untouchable.

The Backup Plan

In the rare case someone challenges you, backtrack gracefully. Say, "I'd be happy to help if someone can walk me through it—I just want to make sure I don't overstep." This makes you seem cooperative, even though your goal is to escape the task entirely.

By claiming "That's above my pay grade," you've unlocked the ultimate workplace escape hatch. You'll look humble, avoid extra work, and maintain the illusion of being a team player. In the corporate jungle, this phrase is your survival tool—wield it wisely!

11. Become "The IT Guy" and Troubleshoot Everyone's Printers—Slowly

Few workplace roles are as oddly revered and universally needed as "the IT guy," especially when it comes to printers. Everyone fears printers—those unpredictable, paper-jamming relics of office life. By becoming the unofficial "printer whisperer," you'll not only avoid your actual work but also gain the admiration of your coworkers for fixing something they don't understand. The trick? Fix it *just slowly enough* to maximize your downtime.

Step 1: Set the Stage

Announce yourself as someone who's "pretty good with tech." Don't claim to be an expert—that will only raise expectations. Instead, drop hints like, "Oh, I've dealt with printer issues before. They're tricky, but I can usually figure them out." Soon, coworkers will come running whenever there's a paper jam or a blinking light.

Step 2: Wait for the First Call
You don't need to seek out printer problems—they'll find you. The moment someone says, "Ugh, the printer isn't working," spring into action. Sigh dramatically and say, "Let me take a look." This is your golden ticket to escape whatever task you were supposed to be doing.

Step 3: Stretch the Diagnosis Phase
When you approach the printer, don't fix it immediately. Instead, stare at it like it's a complex piece of machinery you're encountering for the first time. Press a few random buttons, frown thoughtfully, and mutter things like:
- "Hmm, this is strange."
- "I haven't seen this error code before."
- "Did someone update the drivers recently?"

These phrases buy you time while making it look like you're doing something important.

Step 4: The Fake Fixes
Attempt a few "fixes" that you know won't work, like turning the printer off and on or reloading the paper tray in a needlessly elaborate way. After each failed attempt, nod slowly and say, "That rules out one possibility."

If coworkers hover nearby, encourage them to leave by saying, "This might take a while. I'll let you know when it's working." This clears the area so you can relax without an audience.

Step 5: The Glorious Fix (Eventually)
After a sufficient amount of time has passed—ideally 20 to 30 minutes—finally resolve the issue. (Most printer problems can be solved by unjamming the paper or

selecting the correct print queue, but don't do this too soon.) When the printer starts working again, smile modestly and say, "It wasn't too bad, just a bit tricky."

Optional: Leave the printer partially disassembled, even though it works perfectly. This adds an air of mystery and ensures no one tries to fix it themselves next time.

Step 6: Maintain Your Role
Now that you've established yourself as the office IT guy, future printer issues will automatically come to you. Each new problem is another opportunity to avoid your real responsibilities while looking like a hero.

Advanced Techniques
- Invent a "phantom issue" that requires a software update or a new part, then spend days researching it online.
- Recommend the office consider upgrading to a newer printer model and volunteer to "look into it," which can take weeks of "research."
- Create a troubleshooting checklist that's overly complicated and designed to confuse others so they'll always call you first.

The Backup Plan
If the problem genuinely stumps you, blame the manufacturer. Say something like, "These older models are just finicky. It's probably time for a replacement." This shifts the responsibility to someone else while keeping your reputation intact.

By becoming "the IT guy," you've secured a role that's technically both helpful and unhelpful. With a broken printer at your mercy, you can kill hours at work while everyone else assumes you're the office savior. And really, isn't that better than finishing that report?

12. Develop a Mysterious "Back Issue" That Requires Frequent Stretching Breaks

A mysterious back issue is the perfect excuse to frequently step away from your desk without raising eyebrows. After all, no one questions a health-related problem—especially one as relatable as back pain. By sprinkling your day with "necessary" stretches and exercises, you can avoid work while looking like someone bravely soldiering through discomfort.

Step 1: Establish the Backstory
Casually mention your back pain to a few coworkers. Say something vague but sympathetic, like, "Oh, I tweaked my back a little over the weekend. I think it's just stress or bad posture." This plants the seed of your mysterious ailment. Over time, you can build on this narrative, adding details like, "It's been acting up again lately—probably from all this sitting."

The beauty of this approach is that no one can prove or disprove your back pain. It's invisible, subjective, and universally understood.

Step 2: Announce Your Stretching Regimen
Once your back pain is "established," tell your team you're incorporating stretching breaks into your routine. Frame it as a proactive, health-conscious decision: "My doctor

recommended I take stretching breaks throughout the day. It's really important for spinal health." Bonus points if you mention a specific condition, like sciatica—it sounds official and intimidating.

Step 3: The Stretching Routine
Every hour or so, stand up dramatically and announce, "Time for a quick stretch break!" Then, proceed to do a series of exaggerated stretches in full view of your coworkers. Some effective moves include:

- The **Overhead Reach:** Stand tall, stretch your arms toward the ceiling, and hold for an absurdly long time.
- The **Touch Your Toes (Sort of):** Bend forward like you're reaching for your toes, but don't actually touch them. Sigh audibly as you come back up.
- The **Chair Twist:** Sit sideways in your chair, grab the backrest, and twist. Make it look like you're trying to realign your spine with sheer willpower.

Optional: Add a few yoga poses, like Downward Dog, for extra drama.

Step 4: Take It to the Next Level
For advanced slackers, your stretching breaks can evolve into brief walks around the office or even outside. Announce, "I need to loosen up my back—it's feeling stiff again," and disappear for 10–15 minutes. If questioned, simply say, "Walking helps prevent chronic pain." Who's going to argue with that?

Step 5: Solicit Sympathy
Occasionally drop hints about your back pain to elicit sympathy. Rub your lower back while grimacing slightly or

say things like, "It's manageable, but I just need to stay on top of it." Coworkers will admire your resilience and give you a free pass for any perceived lack of productivity.

Advanced Techniques
- Bring in a heating pad or a lumbar support cushion for your chair. These props make your back pain seem even more believable.
- Reference advice from a "specialist." For example, say, "My physical therapist told me to stand every 30 minutes." (No one will ask for proof.)
- Introduce "ergonomic research" as a side project. Spend hours shopping for standing desks or reading reviews of desk chairs.
- Ask coworkers "have you ever had back pain?" then sit back and listen while you waste 30 minutes, because yes, everyone has had back pain and wants to tell you about it.

The Backup Plan
If someone questions your frequent breaks, respond with a disapproving look and say, "You know, ignoring back pain can lead to serious issues later. I'm just trying to stay healthy." This will guilt them into silence.

By developing a mysterious back issue, you've created a perfectly acceptable reason to interrupt your workday as often as you like. You'll not only avoid tasks but also gain a reputation as someone who prioritizes health and wellness. Stretch your way to freedom—you deserve it!

13. Suggest "Team-Building Activities" Like Trust Falls During Busy Seasons

Nothing derails productivity quite like a well-timed suggestion for team-building activities. The genius of this strategy is its outward appearance of selflessness: you're promoting team cohesion and morale! Meanwhile, everyone—including you—is pulled away from actual work for an hour (or more) of forced bonding. And what's the best time to propose this? During the busiest and most stressful season, of course.

Step 1: Pitch the Idea

Wait until a team meeting or casual conversation when everyone looks particularly overwhelmed. Then, in your most cheerful tone, say something like:

- "I've noticed we've all been super busy lately—wouldn't it be great to take a little time to reconnect as a team?"
- "I think a quick team-building session could really help us recharge and work more effectively."

The key is to position your suggestion as a solution to the stress. No one will dare oppose the idea, lest they look like a killjoy.

Step 2: Propose Trust Falls

Among the many options for team-building activities, trust falls are your secret weapon. They're awkward, time-consuming, and require a lot of setup. Pitch them with enthusiasm: "Trust falls are such a classic way to build confidence in each other. Plus, they're fun!"

Optional: Throw in a fake statistic, like, "Did you know trust-building activities improve team performance by 73%?" No one will fact-check you.

Step 3: Drag Out the Planning Process
Once everyone agrees (or reluctantly nods), volunteer to organize the activity. This is your chance to turn a simple suggestion into a multi-step production. Say things like:

- "We'll need a space with enough room—let me check availability."
- "Should we have a short meeting to discuss ground rules first?"
- "Maybe we can order some snacks—what's everyone's favorite?"

Suddenly, your trust falls have morphed into a half-day extravaganza.

Step 4: Execute the Activity (Slowly)
On the big day, take your time setting up. Rearrange furniture unnecessarily, check imaginary safety hazards, and explain the rules in painstaking detail. Then, as each person participates, offer long, overly detailed feedback like, "Great form, but maybe try falling with a little more trust next time."

If you're feeling bold, feign an exaggerated fear of falling and/or injuring your back further (see number 12 above) so you can spend the activity "mentoring" others rather than participating.

Step 5: Solicit Feedback
After the activity, suggest a feedback session to "reflect on the experience." Stretch this out with open-ended questions like:
- "How did it feel to put your trust in the team?"
- "What did we learn about collaboration today?"
- "How can we apply this to our daily work?"

These questions will eat up even more time while giving the illusion of meaningful engagement.

Advanced Techniques
- Suggest adding a second team-building activity, like an obstacle course or a scavenger hunt, for the next week.
- Bring up trust falls in future meetings as an example of "how we can improve our teamwork."
- Start a discussion about creating a monthly team-building schedule—led by you, of course.
- Suggest a 'team building experience' at an exotic or expensive location. Really push it to see what you can get away with.

The Backup Plan
If anyone complains that the activity wasted time, respond with, "I just thought it was important to invest in our team dynamic. A strong team works better together!" This will guilt them into silence and possibly make them question their priorities.

By introducing trust falls as a crucial team-building activity, you've successfully turned busywork into bonding time. You'll not only dodge your tasks but also gain a reputation as someone who deeply values teamwork. Because sometimes, doing less means *falling* into the perfect excuse.

14. Make Your Slack Status "In a Meeting" Indefinitely

Slack statuses are the modern workplace equivalent of a "Do Not Disturb" sign. By setting your status to "In a Meeting" and leaving it there indefinitely, you can avoid interruptions, questions, and even direct assignments. It's the ultimate workplace cloaking device, allowing you to look busy while doing as little as humanly possible.

Step 1: Set the Status
The key to success is a vague yet professional status. Options include:
- "In a meeting."
- "Deep in focus mode."
- "Reviewing critical reports."

Choose an emoji to accompany your status, like the calendar icon or a pair of glasses, for added credibility. Make sure it's just professional enough to discourage follow-ups but not so detailed that it invites scrutiny.

Step 2: The Permanent Meeting
To make your indefinite "In a Meeting" status believable, occasionally hint at your packed schedule. Casually drop lines in conversation like, "It's been one of those weeks— back-to-back meetings all day!" or "I barely had time to eat lunch with all these meetings."

If anyone asks about your availability, sigh dramatically and say, "I'm booked solid this week, but I'll try to find some time." This creates the illusion that your status reflects a genuine, ongoing commitment.

Step 3: Enforce the Illusion

The beauty of "In a Meeting" is that no one wants to interrupt someone who's presumably dealing with important business. However, just in case, be prepared to field the occasional message. Respond with:

- "Can this wait until later? I'm tied up right now."
- "I'm in a meeting, but let's circle back after."
- "I can't talk now—can you put it in an email?"

These responses are vague enough to buy time while discouraging further inquiries.

Step 4: Live the Lifestyle

To really sell the "In a Meeting" persona, make a habit of disappearing for chunks of time. Go grab a coffee, take a walk, or browse memes—just don't be seen. If you work in an office, commandeer an empty meeting room and stare at your laptop occasionally while sipping your drink. If you work remotely, mute notifications and let your Slack status do the heavy lifting.

Advanced Techniques

For the truly bold, pair your "In a Meeting" status with other activities:

- Share a screenshot of a random Zoom call (it could be from last week) in a team chat and say, "Another productive session!"
- Complain vaguely about "meeting fatigue" to reinforce the idea that you're overbooked.

- Suggest that coworkers send you a written summary instead of discussing things live, claiming, "It's just more efficient with my schedule."
- Once you've directed your co-workers to send everything to you in an email, refer to number 8 above and ignore that email for a week.

The Ultimate Defense
If someone asks why your status is always "In a Meeting," brush it off with:
- "Oh, I forgot to update that—thanks for the reminder!" (and then don't change it).
- "You know how it is—meetings are never-ending these days!"
- "I've been hopping between calls all week. Let me fix that when I get a chance."

They'll likely nod in sympathy and move on, leaving you to your uninterrupted slacking.

By keeping your Slack status set to "In a Meeting," you've created a protective barrier against workplace distractions (or actual work). It's a small, digital act of rebellion that allows you to stay under the radar while projecting an air of constant busyness. You're not just avoiding tasks—you're thriving in the illusion of productivity!

15. Use Lots of Jargon in Emails So No One Understands If You're Actually Working

Nothing confuses (or impresses) coworkers like a well-placed avalanche of corporate jargon. By peppering your emails with vague, buzzword-heavy language, you can obscure the fact that you're doing very little while sounding like a strategic genius. Jargon is your shield, your sword, and your smoke bomb—all in one.

Step 1: Master the Buzzwords
Before you begin, familiarize yourself with the key phrases that will make you sound busy without saying anything of substance. Some all-time classics include:
- "Leverage our core competencies."
- "Synergize cross-functional deliverables."
- "Optimize for scalability."
- "Pivot to a proactive framework."
- "Align with organizational objectives."

Sprinkle these into every email, and people will either assume you're brilliant or be too embarrassed to admit they don't understand you.

Step 2: Overcomplicate Simple Concepts
Turn even the simplest updates into a jargon-filled masterpiece. For example:
- Instead of: "Let's meet to finalize the report."
- Write: "We should coordinate a touchpoint to align on the final iterations of the report deliverables."

See? It's the same thing, but now it sounds important enough to excuse delays.

Step 3: Use Ambiguity to Your Advantage
Jargon is most effective when it leaves room for interpretation. For example:
- "I'll circle back once we've fleshed out the granular details of the initiative."

- "This requires a deeper dive to ensure alignment with key stakeholders."
- "I'm looping in additional context to triangulate the most impactful approach."

These sentences sound like action plans but commit you to nothing.

Step 4: Create a Buzzword Chain Reaction
When responding to an email, respond with even more jargon than the sender used. For example, if someone says, "Can you confirm the timeline for this project?" reply with:

- "Absolutely. I'm currently streamlining the workflow to enhance deliverable timelines while ensuring strategic alignment across teams."

Congratulations—you've completely derailed the conversation, and now *they* have to figure out what to ask next.

Step 5: Use Templates
For maximum efficiency, create a library of jargon-filled email templates you can copy and paste as needed.

Examples:
- **Delaying a Task:** "To ensure this aligns with our overarching objectives, I'm prioritizing a strategic approach to this deliverable and will follow up once the framework is finalized."
- **Dodging Accountability:** "Let's ensure we have buy-in from leadership before moving forward. Happy to support as needed!"

- **Deflecting Questions:** "That's a great point—we should workshop this further to uncover additional insights."

Advanced Techniques
For seasoned jargon artists, take your mastery to the next level:
- Use acronyms no one understands (e.g., "We need to TPI this with the ELT for full ROI alignment").
- Include a chart or diagram that looks complex but is actually meaningless.
- Reply-all with a jargon-packed email, ensuring everyone is equally baffled.

The "I'm Working" Illusion
The best part about this tactic is that no one will dare admit they don't follow what you're saying. Instead, they'll nod in agreement, forwarding your email to others who will also pretend to understand. Your clever use of jargon becomes a shield against follow-ups and a time-wasting maze for everyone else.

The Backup Plan
If anyone calls you out on overcomplicating things, just say, "I was trying to ensure we covered all bases strategically." Then offer to "simplify" your email while secretly adding more jargon to the next one.

By mastering the art of jargon-filled emails, you'll confuse your coworkers, avoid extra work, and gain a reputation as someone who's always "thinking strategically." After all, why work harder when you can just leverage your core competencies?

16. Schedule Unnecessary Meetings, Then Blame Someone Else and Say, "This Could've Been an Email"

Meetings are the perfect way to eat up time without actually doing much—especially when you can shift the blame to someone else for scheduling them. By taking the initiative to schedule an unnecessary meeting, then subtly pointing the finger elsewhere and declaring, "This could've been an email," you'll come out looking like the sensible one while everyone else loses an hour of their day.

Step 1: Set the Stage
Choose a meeting topic that's vague enough to sound like it *might* be important but is ultimately pointless. Examples include:
- "Touching Base on Ongoing Initiatives"
- "Quick Sync on Team Priorities"
- "General Updates: Let's Align"

When scheduling the meeting, keep the description short and uninformative so no one knows what to expect. This adds an air of mystery and ensures everyone attends "just in case."

Step 2: Shift the Blame Early
In your meeting invite, hint that the meeting is someone else's idea. For example:
- "Following up on a suggestion from [insert colleague's name] to touch base on this."
- "Thought it might be helpful to discuss in person after [another person's] email."

- "Based on some feedback, I'm putting time on the calendar for us to align."

This small detail ensures that when the meeting inevitably goes sideways, you're not the one holding the bag.

Step 3: Fill the Room
Invite as many people as possible to create the illusion of collaboration. Include a mix of folks who are only tangentially involved, people who won't contribute, and at least one person who loves to talk in circles. A larger group ensures the meeting drags on longer than necessary.

Step 4: Let Chaos Unfold
When the meeting starts, don't take charge. Instead, open with something like, "I just wanted to make sure we're all on the same page. [Insert scapegoat's name], did you want to kick us off?" Sit back and let confusion reign.
If no one takes the lead, encourage group discussion with vague prompts like:
- "What's everyone's perspective on this?"
- "Does anyone have updates they want to share?"
- "Let's open the floor for thoughts."

This lack of structure ensures the meeting meanders aimlessly, eating up valuable time.

Step 5: The Heroic Declaration
As the meeting sputters to an unproductive close, swoop in with the hero move:
- "You know, now that we've talked this through, I'm realizing this could've been an email. We probably didn't need to meet for this."

Smile apologetically and look around the room as if you're *just as frustrated as everyone else*. People will nod in agreement, blaming the mysterious forces (or the scapegoat) that caused the meeting. Meanwhile, you're off the hook and come across as the voice of reason.

Advanced Techniques
For an extra layer of brilliance:
- Pretend you "only scheduled it because you thought it was important to someone else."
- Suggest next time you "streamline communication" with an email instead of a meeting, making yourself sound proactive and efficient.
- Send out a follow-up email summarizing the meeting but frame it as if someone else insisted on having the discussion.

The Backup Plan
If anyone catches on to your strategy, shrug and say, "I was just trying to help facilitate things—next time, we can definitely skip the meeting." This sounds selfless, even though your true goal was to waste everyone's time.

By scheduling pointless meetings, blaming someone else, and declaring them unnecessary, you've mastered the art of workplace time-wasting with zero accountability. It's not just a tactic; it's a performance. Bravo!

17. "Lose" Important Documents and Spend Hours "Looking" for Them

Few things derail productivity as effectively as misplaced documents—especially when you're the one who "accidentally" lost them. By creating a small-scale office mystery, you'll buy yourself hours of distraction as you pretend to search high and low for the elusive paperwork, all while avoiding your actual tasks.

Step 1: Pick Your Target
Choose a document or file that is moderately important but not urgent enough to raise alarms. This could be:
- A printout of a meeting agenda.
- A shared file you "forgot" to upload to the cloud.
- That report you were supposed to finalize last week.

Whatever it is, make sure it's something that people will expect you to have but won't immediately suspect you of intentionally losing.

Step 2: Create the Illusion of Misplacement
Begin by staging the disappearance. Casually announce to your team, "I had it right here yesterday—I swear! Has anyone seen [insert document name]?" Ruffle through a stack of papers or click aimlessly through your computer files to sell the moment. Bonus points if you furrow your brow and mutter, "I could've sworn I saved it."

Step 3: Expand the Search
Once the missing document becomes a topic of interest, go all-in on the search effort:

- Open and close desk drawers repeatedly, shaking your head dramatically.
- Spend a suspiciously long time searching the same cabinet or folder.
- Ask coworkers if they've seen it, forcing them to get involved.

If you're feeling bold, walk around the office asking, "Who took it? Come on, which one of you is pranking me?", thereby painting yourself as someone well enough liked to be pranked by office friends.

Step 4: Play the Victim
As the search continues, ramp up your frustration to garner sympathy. Say things like:
- "This is so unlike me—I'm usually so organized!"
- "It must've gotten mixed up somewhere. Ugh, what a mess!"
- "I just want to find it so I can move on with my day!"

This deflects suspicion and makes others feel bad for you, even though you're doing absolutely nothing useful.

Step 5: The Convenient Discovery
After an appropriate amount of time has passed (ideally a couple of hours), "find" the document in a place where it was never supposed to be. For example:
- "Oh my gosh, it was in the printer tray this whole time!"
- "Wow, I accidentally saved it in the wrong folder—what are the odds?"
- "Someone must've moved it to this pile without realizing. No harm, no foul!"

Smile sheepishly and apologize to anyone who helped you search, claiming, "I guess my brain's all over the place today!" They'll forgive you instantly because everyone makes mistakes, right?

Advanced Techniques
- If you're dealing with a digital file, claim your computer "didn't save properly" and that you'll need more time to recreate it. This adds an extra layer of delay.
- Suggest a new system to "prevent this from happening again," like reorganizing shared folders or labeling everything. Spend a full day on this instead of actual work.
- If someone gets annoyed, quickly pivot to helping them with their own task, creating a second layer of distraction.

The Backup Plan
If anyone questions your competence after a few too many "lost" documents, shrug and say, "It happens to the best of us—I think we all know how easy it is to misplace things when we're juggling so much!" This reinforces the idea that you're overwhelmed and overworked, earning you sympathy instead of suspicion.

By "losing" important documents and creating an elaborate scavenger hunt, you've found the perfect excuse to waste hours of your day while looking like a diligent problem-solver. Who needs productivity when you've got plausible deniability? Bravo, detective!

18. Offer to Be on the Company Morale Committee, Then Use It to Plan Happy Hours

The company morale committee sounds like a noble endeavor: boosting team spirit, improving workplace culture, and making your office a better place to be. But for you, it's the ultimate excuse to avoid real work while focusing on the "important" task of planning after-hours drinks. After all, nothing builds morale like margaritas.

Step 1: Volunteer Enthusiastically
When the topic of improving office morale comes up, jump at the opportunity to join (or create) the committee. Say things like:
- "I've always been passionate about making work fun!"
- "Team morale is so important—count me in!"
- "I'd love to help make the office a happier place!"

Your eagerness will make you look like a selfless team player, even though your true goal is to spend hours debating the merits of taco bars over karaoke nights.

Step 2: Create Endless Discussions
Once you're on the committee, turn every decision into an unnecessarily drawn-out process. Suggest meetings to "brainstorm" ideas and insist on considering all possibilities before making a final choice. Example discussion topics include:
- "Should we do a pizza party or a potluck?"
- "What's the best day of the week for maximum attendance?"

- "Do we need a theme for this quarter's happy hour?"

These debates will fill meeting after meeting, ensuring you and your fellow committee members stay "busy" without actually accomplishing anything.

Step 3: Focus on Happy Hours
When it's time to propose morale-boosting events, steer every conversation toward happy hours. Use phrases like:
- "Nothing builds camaraderie like drinks after work!"
- "Happy hours are so simple, but they bring everyone together."
- "We can keep it casual, but it'll still feel special!"

Suggest local bars, breweries, or even rooftop spots. Spend hours Googling venues and discussing drink menus under the guise of "research."

Step 4: Turn Planning Into a Full-Time Job
Take your event planning responsibilities to ridiculous lengths. Examples include:
- Polling the entire office about their favorite cocktail.
- Comparing Yelp reviews for 10 different venues.
- Debating the ratio of appetizers to attendees.
- Insisting on personalized drink tickets or branded koozies.

If anyone questions why planning is taking so long, say, "We want to make sure this event really hits the mark!" No one will argue against your "dedication."

Step 5: Execute Slowly
On the day of the event, arrive early to "coordinate logistics" (aka sip a drink while pretending to supervise). Spend the

event chatting about how much effort you put into planning it, and afterward, suggest a debrief meeting to discuss what went well and what could be improved next time.

Advanced Techniques
For seasoned morale committee pros, add these strategies to your repertoire:
- Suggest creating a monthly happy hour schedule and spend weeks fine-tuning it.
- Insist on testing local venues before committing—this means visiting bars during work hours "just to be sure."
- Propose themed events that require elaborate planning, like "Prohibition Speakeasy Night."

The Backup Plan
If someone accuses you of focusing too much on happy hours, defend yourself with:
- "Team morale is priceless—we need these bonding moments!"
- "It's not just about the drinks; it's about building connections."
- "People work better when they feel appreciated!"

By framing your happy hour obsession as a selfless act, you'll emerge as the hero of workplace culture.

By joining the morale committee and focusing solely on happy hours, you've found a way to dodge real work while gaining a reputation as the office fun-maker. Cheers to your brilliance—and another round, please!

19. When Assigned Something, Ask for a "Quick Clarification" About Every Detail

The art of doing less at work is often about turning one task into an exhausting game of 20 Questions. By repeatedly asking for "quick clarifications" on even the simplest assignments, you can stretch out your workday while making it look like you're being thorough. It's the perfect way to appear engaged while subtly avoiding progress.

Step 1: Accept the Task Enthusiastically
When you're first assigned the task, act excited and willing. Say something like, "Of course! I'd love to take this on." This sets the stage for your soon-to-be elaborate questioning spree. It's important to look eager so no one suspects you're planning to drag this out for as long as possible.

Step 2: Start With Basic Questions
Begin with harmless, obvious questions. Examples include:
- "What's the deadline for this?" (Even if they already told you.)
- "Who should I check with if I have questions during the process?"
- "Are there any specific tools or resources you recommend?"

These initial inquiries make you seem proactive and engaged, even though they're just filler to buy you time.

Step 3: Dive Into the Details
Once the basics are covered, move on to overly specific, unnecessary clarifications. For instance:

- "Should I format the report in Arial or Calibri?"
- "Do you want this in a spreadsheet or a Word document?"
- "Would you prefer bullet points or numbered lists for this section?"

These types of questions force your boss or coworker to micromanage the task for you, effectively making them part of the problem.

Step 4: Follow Up With "Just One More Thing"
Every time your questions are answered, come back with one more. Use phrases like:
- "Oh, one last thing I forgot to ask..."
- "Just to clarify, when you said XYZ, did you mean ABC?"
- "I was reviewing my notes and realized I'm not 100% clear on this part."

Each follow-up question resets the clock, giving you yet another delay.

Step 5: Blame Your Attention to Detail
If anyone starts to look annoyed, frame your endless clarifications as a strength. Say something like:
- "I just want to make sure I get this exactly right!"
- "I'd rather ask questions now than have to redo it later."
- "I know I'm being thorough, but I want this to meet your expectations."

No one can fault you for "caring too much" about the quality of your work.

Step 6: Use Their Answers Against Them
Once you've collected enough information, use it to stall
further. For example:
- "I was following up on your earlier suggestion, but
  now I'm wondering if we should take a different
  approach."
- "Based on what we discussed, I think we should
  gather more input before proceeding."
- "I realized there might be a better way to tackle
  this—should I explore that first?"

Each of these excuses kicks the can down the road, giving
you even more time to avoid the actual work.

Advanced Techniques
For seasoned procrastinators, add these tactics to your
arsenal:
- Send your clarifications via email, creating a paper
  trail that makes it look like you're being extra diligent.
- Bring up your questions in team meetings to involve
  even more people in your stalling strategy.
- Revisit previously answered questions to "double-
  check" their accuracy.

The Backup Plan
If anyone calls you out for over-complicating things,
respond with:
- "I just wanted to make sure I wasn't missing anything
  important!"
- "I thought it was better to ask now than risk making a
  mistake later."
- "I was trying to be as thorough as possible for the
  sake of the team."

These excuses make you sound conscientious rather than inefficient, turning your stalling into a virtue.

By asking for constant clarifications, you've mastered the art of appearing proactive while ensuring you accomplish as little as possible. Who knew endless questions could lead to so few answers?

20. Suggest Converting All Tasks Into "Brainstorming Sessions"

Why complete a task when you can gather everyone in a room to "brainstorm" about it first? By proposing brainstorming sessions for every assignment, you create a black hole of endless discussion where no actual work gets done. Better yet, you'll look like a collaborative visionary, even though your real goal is to stall for time and share the workload with the entire team.

Step 1: Suggest a Brainstorm as the "First Step"
When assigned a task, don't dive straight into it. Instead, say something like:
- "I think it'd be great to get everyone's input before we start."
- "This would really benefit from a quick brainstorming session to align ideas."
- "Why don't we get the team together to collaborate on this?"

The key is to frame brainstorming as an essential step that will improve the final product, even though it's just a tactic to delay doing the work yourself.

Step 2: Make It Sound Inclusive

Present brainstorming as a way to value everyone's contributions. Say, "I don't want to miss out on any great ideas from the team." This makes it harder for anyone to decline the session because turning it down makes *them* look like the one who doesn't care about teamwork.

Step 3: Schedule the Session (for Maximum Delay)

Choose a time that's several days away to give everyone "adequate notice." This buys you a few extra days of not starting the task while making it look like you're simply being considerate. For added delay, use scheduling conflicts as an excuse to push the session back even further.

Step 4: Let the Chaos Begin

During the brainstorming session, avoid steering the conversation. Instead, let it spiral into a free-for-all of unrelated ideas and tangents. Encourage this by asking broad, open-ended questions like:

- "What's everyone's vision for this?"
- "What are some out-of-the-box ideas we can explore?"
- "How do we want this to reflect our overall goals?"

The more vague and open-ended your questions, the more time the team will spend talking in circles.

Step 5: Capture "Ideas" Without Commitment

Take notes on every random idea that's thrown out but avoid committing to any concrete actions. Say things like:

- "That's an interesting perspective—we should definitely explore that further."

- "I'll jot that down and see how it fits into the bigger picture."
- "Great idea! Let's keep it on the table for now."

This ensures that nothing actually gets decided, leaving the task right where it started.

Step 6: Propose a Follow-Up Session
When the brainstorming session wraps up without any clear outcomes, suggest another session to "narrow down ideas." This guarantees at least one more meeting where you can continue to avoid making progress.

Advanced Techniques
- Introduce buzzwords like "blue-sky thinking" or "ideation" to make the session sound more important.
- Bring props like sticky notes and markers to make it look interactive and productive, even if nothing gets accomplished.
- Suggest breaking the brainstorming into smaller sub-sessions for different aspects of the task—each requiring its own meeting.

The Backup Plan
If someone grows impatient and asks why the task hasn't moved forward, respond with:
- "We're still in the ideation phase, and I want to make sure we explore all possibilities."
- "It's better to spend more time planning than rushing into something incomplete."
- "This process ensures we're aligned and producing our best work."

These excuses will buy you even more time while making it seem like you're prioritizing quality over speed.

By suggesting brainstorming sessions for everything, you've turned even the smallest tasks into drawn-out group projects. You'll look collaborative and forward-thinking while successfully avoiding the real work. Who needs action when you've got endless ideas? Brilliant strategy, visionary!

21. Spend 45 Minutes Writing the Perfect Three-Sentence Email

Emails are a cornerstone of modern work—and the perfect excuse to waste an absurd amount of time. Why dash off a quick reply when you can spend nearly an hour crafting the perfect three sentences? By pretending every email is a delicate work of art, you can justify an entire morning spent agonizing over word choice, formatting, and punctuation.

Step 1: Set the Scene
When faced with an email that requires a response, open it immediately and then stare at it thoughtfully for a solid ten minutes. Let out a small sigh, as if grappling with the weight of your responsibilities. If anyone glances your way, they'll see someone utterly consumed by the complexities of professional communication.

Step 2: Begin the Draft—Slowly
Start with the greeting. Is "Hi" too casual? Is "Dear" too
formal? Debate this silently with yourself for several
minutes. Type and delete variations like:
- "Hi [Name],"
- "Hello [Name],"
- "Dear [Name],"

Finally settle on one and feel a small sense of
accomplishment. You've already burned 15 minutes.

Step 3: Obsess Over Tone
The body of the email is where the real procrastination
magic happens. Carefully consider every word to strike the
right balance between polite and professional. For example:
- Is "I hope this email finds you well" too generic?
- Does "Let me know if you have questions" sound too
  passive-aggressive?
- Should you end with "Best regards" or just "Best"?

Every sentence is a landmine of potential misinterpretation,
so naturally, you need to rewrite it five or six times.

Step 4: Format Like Your Career Depends on It
Once the content is "perfect," spend an unnecessary
amount of time formatting the email. Should you use bullet
points or numbered lists? Is the font size consistent?
Should you bold the important parts or let them speak for
themselves?

For extra time-wasting, consider adding a hyperlink or
attachment, then double-check that it works. Repeat this
process at least twice.

Step 5: Proofread to Perfection
Now it's time to proofread. Read the email aloud to yourself to ensure it "flows." Check for typos, grammar mistakes, and even redundant commas. This can easily consume another 10 minutes, especially if you start questioning your use of semicolons.

Optional: Open an online grammar tool to confirm that your three sentences meet the highest linguistic standards.

Step 6: Hesitate to Send
Hover over the "Send" button for an unnecessarily long time. Ask yourself:
- "Is this too short?"
- "Did I address everything?"
- "Will they read it the way I intended?"

Finally hit send, then spend five minutes rereading the email in your Sent folder, just in case.

Advanced Techniques
For true procrastinators, take this to the next level by:
- Writing a "draft" version, then rewriting it from scratch.
- Asking a coworker to "take a quick look" at your email for feedback.
- Starting over entirely because you've decided to change the tone.

The Backup Plan
If anyone asks why you've been staring at your screen for so long, respond with:
- "I just wanted to make sure the email was clear and concise."

- "You know how it is—emails are tricky. It's all about tone!"
- "I was triple-checking everything to avoid any misunderstandings."

They'll nod in understanding, perhaps even admiring your "attention to detail."

By spending 45 minutes on a three-sentence email, you've turned a mundane task into a masterpiece of time-wasting. It's not just procrastination—it's a craft. Bravo, email artisan!

22. Bring Donuts to Work So No One Questions Your Productivity (And Everyone Gets a Carb Coma)

When it comes to slacking off at work, a box of donuts is your ultimate power move. Not only does it shield you from suspicion, but the sugar and carb overload will also lull your coworkers into a collective lethargy. By strategically lowering the overall productivity of the office, you can do even less and blend in seamlessly.

Bonus tip: Pizza works wonders for afternoon food comas, too.

Step 1: Announce Your Generosity
Start the day by bursting through the door with the donuts, exuding generosity and charm:
- "Surprise! I thought we could all use a little something sweet this morning."

- "Who's ready to kick off the day with donuts? They're fresh, too!"
- "Figured we needed some extra energy today—donuts for everyone!"

Your coworkers will immediately associate you with good vibes and glazed happiness, distracting them from your lack of actual output.

Step 2: Set the Lethargy Trap
Place the donuts in a high-traffic area, like the breakroom or near the coffee machine. Open the box with a dramatic flourish and encourage everyone to grab one—or two. Engage them in a lively conversation about which flavor is superior. Sprinkle in comments like:
- "It's impossible to say no to sprinkles, isn't it?"
- "Glazed is a classic for a reason. Pure perfection."

Watch as everyone indulges, their energy slowly but surely succumbing to the inevitable sugar crash.

Step 3: Leverage the Mid-Morning Slump
The beauty of donuts lies in their ability to spike energy levels momentarily before sending your coworkers crashing back down. By mid-morning, everyone will be moving slower, complaining about how full they feel, and sneaking in yawns between tasks. This is your time to shine—or rather, to sit quietly and do even less without standing out.

Step 4: Become the Office Favorite
Thanks to the donuts, you'll be seen as the office morale booster, the hero who "just gets it." Nobody will notice you're barely working because the overall productivity level of the office has plummeted. If anyone asks what you're

working on, smile and say, "Just trying to catch up on a few things now that everyone's enjoying the donuts!"

Bonus: Afternoon Pizza Play
If you want to double down on this strategy, propose an impromptu pizza lunch. Offer to "organize" it, then take your time calling around for the best deals and collecting everyone's topping preferences. The heavy carbs from pizza will hit just as the afternoon rolls in, creating a perfect food coma scenario where no one expects much from anyone—including you.

Advanced Techniques
For true masters of workplace laziness:
- Bring in extra sugary donuts like maple bars or Boston creams for maximum lethargy.
- Suggest "taking it slow" today because "we're all in a bit of a food coma."
- Use the donut distraction as an excuse to "step away" and "reset" before diving into tasks—later.

The Backup Plan
If anyone comments on the office-wide slowdown, laugh and say, "Wow, I guess I underestimated the power of donuts!" Your coworkers will agree and thank you for bringing them, effectively silencing any criticism.

By deploying donuts (and pizza for advanced users), you've not only secured goodwill but also cleverly reduced the entire office's productivity to match your own. It's not just slacking—it's strategy. Bravo, carb king!

23. Say, "I'm Still Waiting on Some Data," Even If You're Not

"Waiting on data" is the ultimate excuse for doing nothing while looking like you're in the middle of something crucial. By invoking the mystical powers of delayed information, you can buy yourself endless amounts of time while keeping up the illusion of productivity. After all, who can blame you if your work depends on data that *just hasn't arrived yet*?

Step 1: Lay the Foundation
The key to pulling off this excuse is to establish early on that your task relies on data from someone else. When given an assignment, immediately say, "Great, I'll just need to get some data from [insert department, colleague, or system]." This creates a built-in delay before you've even started.

Step 2: Pick an Elusive Source
Blame your missing data on a source that's notoriously slow or mysterious, such as:
- "I'm waiting on the latest numbers from Finance."
- "IT is supposed to send over the updated metrics."
- "I need the final customer survey results to proceed."

These sources are perfect because no one will want to chase them down for you, and their delays are widely accepted as normal office culture.

Step 3: Bring It Up Casually
Periodically remind your team that you're still in limbo, using vague but confident statements like:

- "I'd love to move forward, but I'm still waiting on the data."
- "The numbers are supposed to come in soon, and then I can really dig in."
- "Once we have the latest metrics, this will all fall into place."

This reinforces the idea that you're ready to work, even though you have no intention of starting anytime soon.

Step 4: Field Questions Like a Pro

If someone asks about your progress, respond with confidence and just a hint of frustration:

- "I'm following up with [data source], but they haven't sent anything yet."
- "I can't make any meaningful progress without the data—it's critical to the process."
- "It's out of my hands until the numbers are in, but I'll be ready when they are."

These statements make it clear that the holdup isn't your fault, and you're just an innocent victim of bureaucracy.

Step 5: Fake Follow-Ups

To maintain the illusion, occasionally pretend to follow up on the missing data. Send an email or Slack message to a generic team alias like "data@company.com" or "financegroup." When no one responds, shrug and say, "I've followed up twice now, but I think they're swamped."

Advanced Techniques

For advanced practitioners of the "waiting on data" excuse:

- Invent a data set that doesn't exist, like "historical Q2-to-Q3 trend analysis."

- Blame software updates or glitches, saying, "The system isn't pulling the data correctly right now."
- Claim the data you received was incomplete or needed "further refinement," giving you even more time.

The Backup Plan
Eventually, someone might grow impatient and ask for an update. If that happens, pivot with:
- "I think we could work on some preliminary ideas while we wait for the final data."
- "Do you think it'd make sense to escalate this to [higher-up]?"
- "I've been thinking about alternative approaches in the meantime—let me share those soon."

This shifts the focus away from the missing data and keeps the task in perpetual limbo.

By claiming you're "still waiting on some data," you've created a foolproof buffer against actual work. With the right amount of confidence and finger-pointing, you'll turn even the simplest task into an extended waiting game. Now sit back and enjoy the downtime—you've earned it!

24. Suggest a New Workflow That Requires Six New Approval Steps

When it comes to doing less at work, nothing slows progress quite like a needlessly complicated workflow. By proposing a "better system" with multiple layers of approvals, you can create a bureaucratic labyrinth that ensures tasks move at a snail's pace—if they move at all. The best part? You'll look like someone who's improving efficiency, even though you're single-handedly grinding productivity to a halt.

Step 1: Identify a Process to Overhaul
Pick a process that seems ripe for "optimization." It could be anything: submitting reports, requesting supplies, or even scheduling meetings. Say something like:
- "I've noticed some inefficiencies in how we handle [process]. I think we could improve it."
- "Our current system is working, but I see an opportunity to streamline things."
- "What if we implemented a more structured workflow for this?"

Your coworkers will nod, grateful that someone (not them) is thinking about process improvement.

Step 2: Propose an Overly Complex Workflow
The key to stalling work is to propose a workflow that looks organized but adds layers of unnecessary complexity. For example:
1. Step 1: Submit an initial draft to the team for review.
2. Step 2: Route the draft to a manager for preliminary approval.
3. Step 3: Have the draft reviewed by a cross-departmental committee.
4. Step 4: Incorporate feedback and resubmit for secondary approval.
5. Step 5: Schedule a meeting to discuss final edits.
6. Step 6: Obtain a formal sign-off from leadership.

By the time the task reaches Step 6, it will be buried under so much red tape that no one will remember what the original goal was.

Step 3: Sell It as a Productivity Booster
Frame your new workflow as a way to improve quality and avoid mistakes. Use phrases like:
- "This ensures we're all aligned before moving forward."
- "A structured process will help us catch any issues early on."
- "The additional steps may take a little extra time, but they'll save us headaches down the road."

Make it sound like you're doing everyone a favor, even though you're just stalling.

Step 4: Insist on a "Trial Run"
Propose a trial period to test the new workflow. This adds even more time to the delay while making it look like you're being thorough. Say things like:
- "Let's pilot this for a month and see how it goes."
- "We'll evaluate the results and tweak the process as needed."
- "I think this will give us some great insights into how to optimize further."

Of course, by the time the trial ends, everyone will be too exhausted to revisit the topic, and your complicated workflow will quietly fade into obscurity.

Step 5: Blame the System for Delays
When coworkers complain that things are moving too slowly, shrug and say:

- "It's just the nature of a thorough process."
- "We're still ironing out the kinks—good workflows take time to perfect."
- "The approval steps are necessary to ensure quality."

This shifts the blame from you to the system you created, shielding you from accountability.

Advanced Techniques
For seasoned procrastinators:
- Suggest adding even more steps during the trial run, such as an "informal pre-review" or a "peer feedback phase."
- Propose a software tool to manage the workflow, then spend weeks researching and demoing options.
- Create detailed flowcharts and diagrams to make the process look so sophisticated that no one dares question it.

The Backup Plan
If leadership pushes back on your workflow, act flexible and say:
- "I just wanted to explore ways to make the process smoother. Happy to simplify it if needed!"
- "I thought this would address some concerns I've heard, but we can always adjust."

This makes you look adaptable, even though you've wasted weeks on a system no one needed.

By suggesting a new workflow with endless approval steps, you've successfully turned even the smallest task into a drawn-out odyssey. Congratulations—you've weaponized inefficiency to do less while looking like a process innovator. Now sit back and watch the gears grind to a halt!

25. Turn Every One-on-One Meeting Into a Conversation About Your Cat

One-on-one meetings are supposed to be a time to discuss work, but who says you have to stick to the agenda? By steering the conversation toward your beloved cat (or any other personal topic), you can waste a significant portion of the meeting talking about fur, whiskers, and the hilarious things your feline did last night. The best part? You'll come across as relatable and charming while avoiding actual work discussions.

Step 1: Set the Stage
As soon as the meeting begins, establish a casual tone. Open with something like:
- "Before we dive in, I have to tell you what my cat did this morning—it was so funny!"
- "You won't believe the new trick my cat just learned."
- "Quick question: Have you ever dealt with a cat who's obsessed with cardboard boxes?"

Your manager or coworker will likely indulge you, thinking it's just a quick aside. Little do they know, this detour is about to become the main event.

Step 2: Build Momentum With Enthusiasm
Once you've broached the subject, go all in. Share detailed anecdotes about your cat's antics:

- "She's started knocking pens off my desk during meetings—like she knows exactly when I'm busy!"
- "I bought her a new toy mouse, and she carries it around like it's her baby."
- "You should've seen her reaction to the vacuum cleaner—it was pure drama!"

Your excitement will draw them in, and before long, they'll be asking follow-up questions, prolonging the conversation even further.

Step 3: Bring Visual Aids
If you're on a video call, have a few cat photos or videos ready to share. Say, "Let me just show you this real quick—it's too good not to share." If your cat happens to wander into the frame, even better! Pick them up and introduce them like a VIP guest: "Oh, here's the star of the story! Say hi to Mr. Whiskers!"

If the meeting is in person, whip out your phone and scroll through your photo gallery. Say, "Sorry, I have to show you this one—it's too cute."

Step 4: Feign Surprise at the Time
When the conversation finally winds down, glance at the clock and feign surprise:
- "Oh wow, we've been talking about cats for 20 minutes! Time flies!"
- "Whoops, I guess I got a little carried away—cats are just so entertaining!"

By then, most of the meeting time will be gone, leaving little room for the actual agenda.

Advanced Techniques

For maximum effectiveness:

- Bring up tangential cat-related topics, like funny pet videos you saw online or the pros and cons of automatic litter boxes.
- Mention your cat's quirky personality traits and ask if they've ever had a pet like that.
- Share "cat advice" you recently read, like the benefits of catnip or tips for grooming.

Expert Level

- You don't even have a cat. You got the cat pictures from the internet. If we're being honest, you don't even like cats.
- If they try to steer the conversation back to the meeting agenda, your cat is now sick. They will be too polite to change the subject.

Bonus: Diversion as a Defense

If the conversation starts veering back toward work, pivot with a question like:

- "By the way, are you a cat person or a dog person?"
- "Do you have any pets? I'd love to hear about them!"

This keeps the discussion personal and away from tasks or deadlines.

The Backup Plan

If someone calls out your cat diversion, respond with playful self-awareness:

- "I know I talk about her too much, but she's basically my little coworker!"
- "Sorry, I guess I've got cats on the brain today. Let's get back to it!"

They'll laugh and move on, likely charmed by your passion for your furry companion.

By turning every one-on-one meeting into a chat about your cat, you've mastered the art of turning professional time into personal storytelling. Not only do you avoid work, but you also boost your office reputation as a relatable, pet-loving human. Pawsitively genius!

26. Start Every Email With, "Apologies for the Delay," Regardless of How Long It Took

Starting every email with "Apologies for the delay" is a brilliant move that simultaneously deflects accountability and lowers expectations for your response times. Whether it's been five minutes, five hours, or five days, this phrase makes you look polite and conscientious—even if you've just been procrastinating the whole time.

Step 1: Make "Apologies for the Delay" Your Default Opener
No matter when you're responding, kick off the email with:
- "Apologies for the delay—thanks for your patience!"
- "Sorry for not getting back to you sooner, I've been swamped."
- "Thanks for your understanding; it's been a bit hectic on my end."

This immediately disarms the recipient, making them feel guilty for even thinking about your tardiness.

Step 2: Blame "Busyness" (Real or Imagined)
Even if your schedule has been wide open, drop hints that you've been buried under an avalanche of work. Say things like:
- "I've been juggling a few deadlines, but I wanted to circle back on this."
- "It's been a bit chaotic, but I'm catching up now!"
- "I appreciate your patience—it's been one of those weeks."

These phrases create the impression that you're doing your best in impossible circumstances, even if your main obstacle was deciding what to have for lunch.

Step 3: Keep the Reply Vague
To minimize follow-ups, keep your response as noncommittal as possible while still sounding engaged. For example:
- "Let me take another look at this and circle back to you shortly."
- "Great point—let me touch base with the team and follow up."
- "I'm reviewing this now and will have an update soon."

This buys you even more time while making it seem like you're actively working on the issue.

Step 4: Turn the Delay Into a Positive
For extra flair, frame your delayed response as a benefit to the conversation. For instance:
- "Taking some time to reflect on this, I think [vague idea] could be the way to go."

- "Thanks for your patience—it gave me a chance to really think this through."
- "I wanted to ensure I had all the details before responding."

This transforms your procrastination into a sign of thoughtfulness.

Step 5: Repeat As Needed
Whenever someone follows up, simply reply with another "apologies for the delay" and restart the cycle. This phrase is a never-ending get-out-of-jail-free card for slow responses.

Advanced Techniques
For seasoned delay-apologizers:
- Add some personalization, like: "Sorry for the delay—your email deserves a thoughtful response!"
- Use an emoji for extra charm.
- Blame technology: "My email has been acting up, but I'm catching up now!"

The Backup Plan
If someone confronts you about how long it took to respond, lean into self-deprecation:
- "I've been buried under emails this week—it's like Whac-A-Mole in my inbox!"
- "I need to work on my response times—thanks for bearing with me!"
- "I'm a little behind, but I promise I'm on it now!"

They'll laugh or nod sympathetically, forgetting all about the delay.

By making "Apologies for the delay" your go-to phrase, you've unlocked the ultimate email stalling tactic. You'll maintain a veneer of professionalism while comfortably dragging your feet—and no one will be the wiser. Slow and steady wins the race!

27. Always Have a Post-it Note in Hand—It Makes You Look Busier

Carrying a Post-it note is the workplace equivalent of wearing a superhero cape. This simple, sticky piece of paper transforms you into someone perpetually on the move, tackling urgent tasks and solving big problems. The best part? No one will stop to check what's written on it—if anything is written at all.

Step 1: Pick Your Post-it
Choose a standard-size Post-it note in a professional yet eye-catching color. Bright yellows, blues, or greens are perfect—they say, "I'm organized, but not boring." For bonus points, add a few scribbles, like a random phone number or the word "deadline," to give the illusion of importance.

Step 2: Carry It Everywhere
Make it a habit to always have the Post-it in hand, whether you're walking to the printer, heading to a meeting, or even grabbing coffee. Grip it loosely between your thumb and forefinger, as if you're about to complete a mission-critical task. If anyone glances at it, hold it closer to your chest and mutter, "Just wrapping this up," before briskly walking away.

Step 3: Look Distracted and Focused

Perfect the art of the distracted-yet-determined expression. Occasionally glance at the Post-it as if decoding a secret message. Furrow your brow slightly, nod as if making mental calculations, and mutter something like, "Okay, just need to check one thing." This makes you look so busy no one will dare interrupt.

Step 4: Use It as a Universal Excuse

The Post-it is your golden ticket to escape any situation. Examples:

- **If someone asks for help:** Hold up the note and say, "Sorry, can't right now—need to finish this first."
- **If your boss asks for a progress update:** Glance at the Post-it and reply, "It's all here, just finalizing a couple of things."
- **If someone wants to chat:** Wave the note vaguely and say, "Can we talk later? I'm in the middle of this."

The vague importance of the note will keep people from asking too many questions.

Step 5: Refresh the Illusion

Every so often, swap out the Post-it for a fresh one to maintain your cover. Write something cryptic like "Follow-up" or "Call at 2:30," even if it's completely meaningless. If anyone catches you recycling Post-its, laugh and say, "I go through these things like crazy—can't stay organized without them!"

Advanced Techniques

For maximum effect:

- Pair your Post-it with a pen, occasionally jotting something down while nodding thoughtfully.

- Stick it to your monitor or desk where others can see it, creating an aura of productivity even when you're scrolling social media.
- Use multiple Post-its layered together, as if you're juggling several high-priority tasks.

The Backup Plan
If someone asks why you're always carrying a Post-it note, shrug and say:
- "It's how I stay on top of things. The second I stop using these, something slips through the cracks."
- "I'm a visual thinker—writing it down keeps me focused."
- "It's my system—works better than any app I've tried!"

No one will argue with your dedication to old-school productivity tools.

By wielding a simple Post-it note, you've created a portable shield against interruptions and work expectations. It's not just stationery—it's a lifestyle. Stick to it, and you'll master the art of looking busy while doing absolutely nothing. Bravo, productivity ninja!

28. Use "I'm Waiting on an Email" to Justify Sitting at Your Desk Doing Nothing

Few excuses are as flexible and foolproof as "I'm waiting on an email." By claiming you're in limbo until that all-important message arrives, you can spend hours at your desk scrolling, daydreaming, or pretending to type while dodging any real work. No one will question you, because *of course* you're just being responsible and "staying on top of things."

Step 1: Set the Scene
Plant the seed early by mentioning the email to coworkers or your boss:
- "I sent a request earlier and just need the response to move forward."
- "I'm waiting for confirmation from [vague department or client]."
- "As soon as I get the email back, I can dive into the next step."

This frames your idle time as strategic, not slacker behavior.

Step 2: Look Busy at Your Desk
While "waiting," maintain an air of focus by:
- Staring intently at your screen as if reading something critical.
- Typing sporadically, even if it's just nonsense or a message draft you'll never send.
- Clicking between open tabs to create the illusion of multitasking.

Occasionally glance at your phone or your email inbox with a frustrated sigh, as if the delay is *really* slowing you down.

Step 3: Deflect With the Email Excuse
When someone asks what you're working on or tries to assign you something else, respond with:
- "I'm on standby until I get this email—don't want to start something else and lose focus."

- "Just waiting on some info before I can finalize things."
- "The minute it hits my inbox, I'll be all over it!"

This keeps the spotlight off you while positioning you as a diligent team player.

Step 4: Extend the Wait Time
If too much time passes and the email hasn't "arrived," add layers to the excuse:
- "They must be swamped—I'll follow up shortly."
- "I think there's been a delay on their end. Shouldn't be much longer."
- "It's probably in their drafts—they're usually good about replying eventually."

Each excuse buys you more time to avoid actual tasks.

Step 5: Claim Victory (or Blame Technology)
When it's time to move on, wrap up your excuse with a plausible resolution:
- "Finally got it—now I can get started."
- "Turns out it went to my spam folder. Classic!"
- "I just followed up, and they said they'll get back to me later—so I'll jump on this tomorrow."

These endings close the loop without requiring you to actually accomplish anything.

Advanced Techniques
For email-waiting experts:
- Pretend to "write a follow-up email" while actually typing nothing important.

- If anyone asks who you're waiting on, pick a vague department: "Oh, it's from IT/Finance—they always take a while."
- Occasionally refresh your inbox dramatically while muttering, "Come on, come on..." to sell the illusion.

The Backup Plan
If someone catches you clearly doing nothing, counter with:
- "I'm just staying ready for when that email comes through—I don't want to miss it."
- "I figured I'd use this downtime to mentally prep for the task."
- "Email delays are the worst—I'm doing my best to keep things moving despite the holdup."

These responses keep you looking proactive while neatly sidestepping responsibility.

By using "I'm waiting on an email" as your go-to excuse, you've mastered the art of looking busy while doing nothing at all. You're not just sitting there—you're holding the digital world together, one nonexistent email at a time. Bravo, inbox magician!

29. Set Your Out-of-Office Reply to "Urgent Matters Only" While Sitting at Your Desk

Out-of-office (OOO) replies aren't just for vacations— they're the ultimate tool for creating a force field of inaccessibility. By setting your OOO reply to "urgent matters only" while you're still at your desk, you can deflect

most emails, avoid follow-ups, and free yourself to do...
well, whatever you want. The best part? People will assume
you're swamped with something far more important.

Step 1: Craft the Perfect OOO Reply

Write an out-of-office message that conveys urgency while
maintaining professionalism. Some examples include:

- "I'm currently out of the office and will be responding
  only to urgent matters. For all other inquiries, I'll get
  back to you as soon as possible."
- "Due to high-priority projects, I'm only available for
  time-sensitive requests. Thank you for your
  patience!"
- "I'm temporarily unavailable but will review emails at
  my earliest convenience. Please contact [generic
  team alias] for immediate assistance."

Make it sound serious, but vague enough that no one can
question why you're unavailable.

Step 2: Set It and Forget It

Turn on the OOO reply even though you're physically in the
office or logged in remotely. This instantly creates the
illusion that you're preoccupied with something critical. If
you're really feeling bold, include a timeframe like, "I'll
return on [future date]," to extend the cover for multiple
days.

Step 3: Act the Part

While your OOO reply is active, lean into the role of
someone who's overwhelmed with important
responsibilities. Wear a focused expression, keep a stack of
papers or open tabs nearby, and occasionally mutter
phrases like:

- "So many moving pieces right now."
- "I'll get to that, but it's going to be a tight squeeze."
- "Deadlines are relentless this week!"

If anyone questions your availability, simply gesture at your screen or calendar with an exasperated sigh.

Step 4: Enjoy Your Freedom
With your OOO reply filtering your inbox, you'll have fewer emails to deal with—and plenty of time to slack off. Spend your day catching up on your favorite series, shopping for new office supplies, or crafting elaborate excuses for other tasks you're avoiding.

Step 5: Handle the Follow-Ups
For the handful of people who bypass your OOO and email you anyway, respond selectively. Use phrases like:
- "Thanks for reaching out—this seems urgent, so I'll prioritize it." (Then don't.)
- "I'm tied up with a high-priority project, but I'll try to address this soon."
- "Let's touch base on this later when my bandwidth improves."

This keeps your inbox manageable while maintaining the facade of being overworked.

Advanced Techniques
For the experienced OOO strategist:
- Include a redirect in your OOO reply: "For urgent matters, contact [team email]." This shifts the burden onto someone else while you stay "busy."

- Add a personal touch like, "I'm currently in back-to-back meetings," to make it sound even more believable.
- Set a recurring calendar event titled "Strategic Priorities" during your OOO period to further justify your inaccessibility.

The Backup Plan
If someone confronts you about why your OOO is on when you're clearly at your desk, respond with:
- "Oh, I set it up because I'm focusing on a critical project and can't afford distractions."
- "It's to help manage expectations—I don't want to miss anything urgent."
- "I must've forgotten to turn it off! Let me fix that after I wrap this up." (Spoiler: You won't fix it.)

By setting your out-of-office reply to "urgent matters only," you've created a digital barrier against work without leaving your chair. It's a simple yet masterful way to control your inbox—and your day. You're not just avoiding tasks; you're optimizing your priorities. Well played!

30. Propose a "Quick Sync" That Turns Into an Hour of Talking About Nothing

The "quick sync" is one of the most versatile tools in the art of doing less at work. It sounds efficient, collaborative, and time-sensitive, but in reality, it's a license to waste an hour rehashing vague ideas without producing anything actionable. Even better, you can spread the responsibility (or blame) to everyone in the room.

Step 1: Propose the Sync
Pick a task that's small enough to not need a meeting but important enough that no one will question your suggestion. Send a message like:
- "Hey, let's schedule a quick sync to align on this."
- "It might be good to get everyone together for a brief discussion."
- "I just want to make sure we're on the same page— how about a quick sync?"

Your coworkers will agree because "quick sync" implies minimal commitment. Little do they know, it's anything but.

Step 2: Gather the Crowd
Invite as many people as possible under the guise of collaboration. Include stakeholders who are only loosely connected to the task, random team members, and at least one person who loves to go on tangents. The larger the group, the less likely anything will get done.

Optional: Use vague language in the invite, like "catching up" or "brainstorming ideas," to keep expectations low and the agenda non-existent.

Step 3: Start With an Open-Ended Question
Kick off the meeting with a broad question that invites rambling, such as:
- "What are everyone's thoughts on this so far?"
- "How do we see this fitting into our overall goals?"
- "Does anyone have any concerns we should address before moving forward?"

This ensures the conversation spirals into irrelevant topics while you sit back and "facilitate."

Step 4: Embrace the Tangents
As the sync devolves into random discussions, encourage them. Use phrases like:
- "That's an interesting perspective—let's explore that for a bit."
- "I hadn't thought of that angle—what does everyone else think?"
- "This is a great conversation—let's keep going."

The longer people talk, the more time you've successfully wasted.

Step 5: Avoid Conclusions
When the meeting starts winding down, skillfully avoid wrapping things up. Instead, say:
- "We've had a lot of great ideas today—I think we need more time to refine them."
- "Let's take these thoughts and regroup later with a clearer direction."
- "This has been really productive; let's table the rest for a follow-up sync."

By deferring decisions to a future meeting, you guarantee the cycle of inefficiency continues.

Advanced Techniques
For seasoned "sync" pros:
- Bring up tangential topics, like "How does this align with our long-term vision?" to derail progress further.
- Suggest creating a shared document to "capture everyone's input," which adds an extra layer of busywork.

- Schedule the sync for a time slot that overlaps with lunch or the end of the day, ensuring everyone is too tired or hungry to make decisions.

The Backup Plan
If anyone questions the purpose of the sync, respond with:
- "I just thought it'd be helpful to get everyone aligned—it's better to over-communicate than under-communicate."
- "I think the discussion itself was valuable, even if we didn't land on a final decision."
- "Sometimes the process of syncing is just as important as the outcomes!"

These statements make it seem like you're prioritizing collaboration, even though you've accomplished nothing.

By proposing a "quick sync" that turns into an hour of talking about nothing, you've created the ultimate workplace time sink. Everyone leaves feeling vaguely productive, while you've skillfully avoided making progress. Sync well, slacker extraordinaire!

31. Blame "System Updates" for Missing Deadlines

System updates are the unsung heroes of the workplace slacker's toolkit. They're mysterious, technical, and entirely believable as a reason for falling behind. Whether it's a real update or one you've completely invented, this excuse buys you time, sympathy, and the perfect opportunity to avoid accountability for missed deadlines.

Step 1: Set the Stage Early
Plant the seed of your excuse by casually mentioning system updates before you even need them. Drop comments like:

- "Did anyone else notice their system running slower today? I think IT pushed an update."
- "My computer just restarted out of nowhere— must've been an update."
- "Looks like there's a patch installing; hopefully, it won't take too long."

This builds a foundation of plausibility, so no one questions your story when things inevitably go "wrong."

Step 2: Deploy the Excuse Strategically
When you're approaching a deadline you'd rather avoid, send an update like this:

- "Just a heads-up: My system is running an update, and it's taking longer than expected."
- "I was about to wrap this up when my computer restarted for a patch installation. I'll need a little more time."
- "Unfortunately, IT updates have slowed me down— should have this done soon once everything stabilizes."

These phrases sound like you're still trying to be productive despite the "setback," earning you extra points for effort.

Step 3: Add Technical Jargon
To make your excuse sound even more legitimate, throw in some technical terms that most people won't question. Examples include:

- "The update is optimizing drivers, so things are running slower than usual."
- "It's a major security patch—looks like it's rewriting system files."
- "I'm stuck at 85% on the update; hopefully, it finishes soon."

The more jargon you use, the less likely anyone will challenge your story.

Step 4: Play the Frustrated Victim
Channel your inner IT novice and act like you're genuinely annoyed by the update. Complain just enough to make it seem like you're trying your best, despite the circumstances:
- "This is so frustrating—I was making good progress until this update hit."
- "Why do these updates always happen at the worst time?"
- "I've already restarted twice; fingers crossed this fixes the issue."

Your coworkers will nod sympathetically, grateful it's you dealing with the inconvenience and not them.

Step 5: Follow Up With a "Recovery Period"
Once you've bought yourself more time, extend the delay by claiming the update caused lingering issues. Say things like:
- "Everything's back up, but my files are taking a while to sync."
- "The system seems stable now, but I need to double-check everything to make sure nothing was lost."
- "Just doing a quick reset to make sure the update didn't corrupt anything."

These excuses buy you even more time to procrastinate.

Advanced Techniques
For expert-level slackers:
- Blame a specific tool or software: "The update messed with my spreadsheet macros, so I need to rebuild a few things."
- Use fake screenshots of "install progress" as visual proof. A quick image search will provide plenty of believable examples.
- Rope in IT by claiming, "I've already submitted a ticket, but they haven't gotten back to me yet."

The Backup Plan
If someone pushes back on your excuse, respond with:
- "I'm just as frustrated as you are—it's completely out of my control."
- "I think IT underestimated how disruptive this update would be. I'll try to escalate it."
- "It's almost resolved—thank you for your patience while I get this sorted!"

These statements deflect blame while reinforcing the idea that you're doing your best under challenging circumstances.

By blaming "system updates" for missing deadlines, you've crafted an excuse that's as believable as it is effective. It's not just procrastination—it's technical strategy. Update complete, slacker supreme!

32. Volunteer to "Document the Process" for a Task, Then Spend Days Writing Absolutely Nothing

Offering to "document the process" is the ultimate way to look helpful while doing almost nothing. It's the kind of task that sounds important, but everyone secretly dreads doing. By volunteering for this noble duty, you can dodge real work, claim you're contributing, and stretch the task out for as long as humanly possible—all while producing little to no actual documentation.

Step 1: Volunteer with Enthusiasm
When a team task comes up that involves any process or workflow, immediately say:
- "I can document this—it'll be helpful for everyone in the future."
- "Let me write it up so it's clear for the team."
- "I'll handle the documentation so we have a solid reference going forward."

Your coworkers will thank you profusely because you've just taken a task off their plates. Little do they know, you're about to take it off yours too.

Step 2: Stretch the Research Phase
Start by saying you need to "fully understand the process" before documenting it. Spend days asking questions, sitting in on meetings, and observing workflows without ever actually writing anything. Use phrases like:
- "I want to make sure I capture every detail accurately."

- "I'm still clarifying a few steps to ensure nothing's missed."
- "This process is more complex than it seems—I need more time to break it down."

These excuses buy you ample time to stall.

Step 3: Claim You're "Organizing the Structure"
Once people start asking about your progress, say you're working on the structure of the document. Talk about how you're debating the best format:
- "Should this be a step-by-step guide or a flowchart?"
- "I'm deciding between a bullet point list or a more narrative format."
- "I'm trying to figure out how to make this user-friendly."

The vagueness of "organizing the structure" ensures no one can measure your progress—or lack thereof.

Step 4: Create a Placeholder Document
To appear like you're making progress, open a blank Word or Google Doc and add a title like "Process Documentation Draft." Share it with the team and say, "This is just a starting point—I'll flesh it out as we go." Leave it mostly empty except for a few generic headings like "Step 1" or "Overview."

Optional: Add a watermark that says "DRAFT" to make it look more official while discouraging anyone from asking questions about its incomplete state.

Step 5: Schedule a Feedback Loop
Suggest a meeting to "review the draft" with the team. Use this opportunity to ask for everyone's input, ensuring that the conversation derails into a long debate about minor details. Say things like:

- "Do we need to include every possible exception, or just the main steps?"
- "What's the best way to word this for clarity?"
- "Does anyone have examples from other teams we could reference?"

The longer the feedback session lasts, the less time you'll have to actually complete the document.

Advanced Techniques
For expert-level process documenters:

- Claim you're running into "version control issues" and need more time to align everything.
- Blame software limitations, saying, "The formatting tools aren't working as expected—I'm troubleshooting."
- Propose adding a visual component (like a diagram) that you'll "work on next week."

The Backup Plan
If someone presses you for a finished document, reply with:

- "I want to get this just right before finalizing it."
- "I'm still gathering input to make sure it's comprehensive."
- "This is a living document—I'll keep updating it as we go."

These responses make it seem like you're prioritizing quality over speed, even if you're prioritizing neither.

By volunteering to "document the process," you've secured a task that's easy to prolong indefinitely while appearing crucial to the team's success. Congratulations—you've mastered the art of productive procrastination. Document that victory!

33. Spend Hours "Testing" Different Fonts for a Presentation

Fonts are the unsung heroes of office presentations, and choosing the perfect one is an art form—or at least, that's the excuse you'll use to delay doing anything else. By claiming you're fine-tuning the look of your slides, you can stretch a 10-minute task into an all-day deep dive into typography. After all, how can anyone argue against the importance of aesthetic perfection?

Step 1: Announce Your Mission
When tasked with creating a presentation, kick things off with an air of gravitas. Say something like:
- "I want to make sure the design really pops—choosing the right font is key."
- "This needs to be visually engaging; I'll spend some time finding the perfect look."
- "Typography can make or break a presentation, so I'm prioritizing that first."

Your coworkers will nod, grateful that someone (not them) cares so deeply about design.

Step 2: Dive Into Font Exploration
Open your presentation software and scroll endlessly through the font menu. Experiment with everything from "Arial" to "Papyrus," even if you know they're terrible choices. Spend 20 minutes testing whimsical options like Comic Sans just to see how bad they look, then another 20 convincing yourself *maybe* they're not that bad.

Optional: Download additional fonts from the internet to expand your options. Bonus points if you spend hours debating whether "Baskerville" is too formal or "Lobster" is too playful.

Step 3: Test Fonts on Every Slide
Apply different fonts to every slide, then step back and "evaluate the overall flow." Ask yourself questions like:
- "Does this font convey professionalism or creativity?"
- "Are these titles bold enough to grab attention?"
- "Should I use the same font for headers and body text, or mix it up?"

Go through this process slide by slide, tweaking each font size and style until you've successfully burned through half your day.

Step 4: Solicit Feedback (and More Opinions)
For maximum delay, ask for feedback from a coworker:
- "Hey, do you think this font works for the tone of the presentation?"
- "Should I go with something modern like Helvetica or stick to a classic like Times New Roman?"
- "What's your opinion on serif fonts for slides? Too old-school?"

Their input will inevitably lead to more options to explore, prolonging your font quest even further.

Step 5: Blame the Fonts for Delays
When asked about your progress, respond with:
- "I'm still finalizing the visual style—getting the fonts right is taking longer than expected."
- "The font I originally wanted doesn't look great on the slides, so I'm testing alternatives."
- "I'm making sure the design is polished before moving on to the content."

These excuses make it seem like you're prioritizing quality and presentation, even though you've barely started the actual work.

Advanced Techniques
For seasoned font fanatics:
- Debate font pairings: "Does Open Sans pair well with Georgia, or is it too jarring?"
- Experiment with kerning and line spacing to further extend the process.
- Suggest that the team choose a "brand font" and schedule a separate meeting to discuss it.

The Backup Plan
If someone grows impatient, pivot with:
- "I wanted the fonts to complement the message— it's almost there!"
- "Design is important for engagement—trust me, this will pay off."
- "I'm wrapping up the visuals today, so the rest should come together quickly."

These responses make you seem detail-oriented rather than distractible.

By spending hours "testing" fonts for a presentation, you've turned procrastination into an art form. You're not just avoiding work—you're fine-tuning the visual experience. Bask in your brilliance, typographic master!

34. Use a Mouse Jiggler to Appear "Active" While Doing Absolutely Nothing

Mouse jigglers are the ultimate tool for workplace slacking, giving you the freedom to step away from your desk while your computer maintains the illusion of nonstop productivity. By keeping your status "active" in chat tools or remote work systems, you can dodge suspicion and take long breaks—all thanks to a tiny, magical gadget.

Step 1: Acquire the Jiggler
Invest in a mouse jiggler—an inexpensive device that gently moves your mouse at random intervals to prevent your computer from going idle. For an even sneakier option, download a mouse-jiggling software program that runs quietly in the background.

Once set up, you've created a tireless digital assistant that ensures your status always says "Available," even if you're miles away or binge-watching your favorite show.

Step 2: Set the Scene
To sell the illusion of productivity, arrange your desk as if you've been in the middle of something important. Keep a spreadsheet, document, or project management tool open on your screen. Scatter a few sticky notes with cryptic scribbles around your workspace for good measure.
If you're on a video call, place your chair slightly out of frame so it looks like you've just stepped away "briefly."

Step 3: Take Advantage of "Active" Status
While your mouse jiggler does its thing, use your newfound freedom wisely:
- Go make a snack or brew coffee.
- Take a long walk or run errands.
- Read, nap, or relax—anything but work.

The key is to return periodically to glance at your screen, adjust a window, or type a few meaningless keystrokes so it looks like you're actively engaged.

Step 4: Blame "Deep Focus"
If someone questions why you didn't respond to messages despite your status being active, blame your dedication to focus:
- "Sorry, I was deep into a project and didn't notice the ping."
- "I must've missed that while reviewing some data— what's up?"
- "My notifications were muted while I was concentrating on this task."

These responses make you seem hardworking and attentive, even though your mouse was doing all the work.

Step 5: Lean Into "Technical Glitches"
For added deniability, claim the jiggler's activity is a tech quirk:
- "Oh, weird—my status must've stayed active while I stepped away for a second."
- "Sometimes my system doesn't update idle time properly; I'll look into it."
- "I thought I set it to 'away,' but maybe it didn't register."

These excuses deflect suspicion while maintaining your cover.

Advanced Techniques
For mouse jiggler masters:
- Pair the jiggler with automated emails or Slack responses to complete the illusion of engagement.
- Set up a second monitor showing charts or documents to make your "active" status seem even more plausible.
- Occasionally check in with coworkers, saying, "Just making sure you're all good—I've been heads-down on this task!"

The Backup Plan
If your jiggler usage is ever discovered, pivot with:
- "It's for preventing my computer from locking during long uploads/downloads."
- "It helps during presentations or screen-sharing to avoid interruptions."
- "I use it to test how idle time impacts our system— pretty insightful, actually!"

These explanations make you look resourceful and tech-savvy, not lazy.

By using a mouse jiggler, you've turned the concept of "active" status into an art form. While your coworkers wonder how you're so consistently engaged, you're living your best stress-free life. Congratulations—you've truly outsmarted the system!

35. Use Phrases Like "We Need to Think Outside the Box" Without Offering Any Ideas

Nothing says "team player" like calling for innovation without contributing a single idea. By peppering meetings with vague motivational phrases like "We need to think outside the box," you can sound like a thought leader while avoiding any actual thinking. It's the ultimate way to look visionary without lifting a finger.

Step 1: Pick the Right Moment
Wait until the conversation reaches a point where people are stuck or circling the same ideas. Then, confidently say:
- "We need to think outside the box on this one."
- "Let's challenge the status quo and come up with something fresh."
- "What if we approached this from a completely new angle?"

Your coworkers will nod in agreement, grateful someone has "elevated" the discussion—even though you've contributed nothing concrete.

Step 2: Avoid Specifics
The key to this strategy is staying as abstract as possible.
Resist the urge to follow up with an actual suggestion.
Instead, keep the focus on the need for creativity:
- "I feel like we're missing a big opportunity here—let's dig deeper."
- "There's got to be a better way to approach this—we just need to find it."
- "I'm sure the solution is out there if we push ourselves to think differently."

This keeps the ball in everyone else's court while you bask in the glow of sounding visionary.

Step 3: Encourage Others to Brainstorm
Once you've delivered your inspirational soundbite, shift the responsibility to your teammates. Use phrases like:
- "What are some outside-the-box ideas we can explore?"
- "I'd love to hear everyone's thoughts on how we can innovate here."
- "Let's open the floor—what comes to mind when we think about fresh approaches?"

This ensures the pressure is off you while the rest of the team scrambles to fill the void.

Step 4: Praise Other People's Ideas
When someone finally offers a suggestion, respond enthusiastically:
- "Now *that's* the kind of outside-the-box thinking I'm talking about!"
- "Exactly! That's the direction we need to go."

- "Great idea—I think we're starting to crack this open."

This makes it look like you were fostering creativity all along, even though you contributed nothing but vague encouragement.

Step 5: Repeat as Needed
If the meeting drifts back into familiar territory, simply reiterate your mantra:
- "I feel like we're slipping back into conventional thinking—let's push the boundaries a bit more."
- "Remember, this is about thinking differently. Let's keep exploring."
- "We're on the right track, but I still think there's room for more innovation."

Each repetition buys you more time without adding any substance to the discussion.

Advanced Techniques
For seasoned idea-avoidance pros:
- Use buzzwords like "blue-sky thinking" or "paradigm shift" to sound extra insightful.
- Suggest breaking into smaller groups to brainstorm, ensuring you can disappear into a quieter corner.
- Propose setting up a follow-up meeting to "dive deeper into creative solutions," effectively kicking the can down the road.

The Backup Plan
If someone calls you out for not offering ideas, pivot with:
- "I'm just trying to create space for everyone's creativity to shine."

- "I didn't want to dominate the discussion—I'm more focused on facilitating."
- "I'm still processing the conversation and will share my thoughts once they're more refined."

These responses position you as a thoughtful collaborator, even though you've contributed zilch.

By using phrases like "We need to think outside the box" without offering ideas, you've mastered the art of workplace sleight-of-hand. You're not just avoiding work—you're inspiring others to do it for you. Bravo, creative genius!

36. Get Away With Not Listening During Meetings by Suggesting "We Need to Drill Down" or "Take a 30,000-Foot View"

Meetings are the perfect time to perfect the art of appearing engaged while not paying attention. By suggesting either "we need to really drill down" or "are we getting too granular? Let's take a 30,000-foot view," you can sound insightful while dodging any responsibility for understanding what's going on. These phrases work like a charm no matter where the conversation is—or how much of it you missed.

Step 1: Identify the Right Moment
Wait for a lull in the meeting when people are debating a point or wrapping up a discussion. If you haven't been listening, you're probably unsure where the conversation is headed. No problem—this is your moment to swoop in with a strategic, all-purpose suggestion.

Step 2: Pick Your Phrase
Choose your tactic based on the meeting's tone (or at random if you have no idea what's happening):

- **Option A: Drill Down**
  Use this when you want to make it sound like the team needs to focus on details:
  - "I think we need to drill down on this to really get to the root of the issue."
  - "Let's take a deeper dive into the specifics to ensure we're covering all our bases."
  - "Before moving on, I feel like we should drill down a bit further here."
- **Option B: 30,000-Foot View**
  Deploy this when you think the discussion might need "refocusing" or more strategy:
  - "I wonder if we're too in the weeds—maybe we should step back and take a 30,000-foot view of this."
  - "Let's consider the bigger picture to ensure we're aligned strategically."
  - "I feel like we're missing the forest for the trees—let's zoom out for a moment."

Both approaches sound equally insightful and can be applied to virtually any situation.

Step 3: Sit Back and Watch the Magic
Once you've thrown out your phrase, the meeting will naturally pivot. The team will either:

1. Start debating the need for more detail (if you suggested drilling down).
2. Discuss the broader implications of the topic (if you proposed zooming out).

Either way, the spotlight shifts away from you, giving you more time to zone out or come up with your next vague contribution.

Step 4: Pretend to Take Notes

To sell the illusion of engagement, nod thoughtfully and jot down random words or doodles in your notebook while the team spins their wheels on your suggestion. Occasionally say things like:

- "That's a great point."
- "I hadn't thought of it that way before."
- "Exactly what I was hoping we'd get into."

These affirmations reinforce the idea that you're a key participant without requiring any real effort.

Advanced Techniques

For expert-level disengagers:

- Use both phrases in the same meeting, switching tactics halfway through: "We've drilled down a lot—maybe now it's time to step back and take a wider view."
- Suggest forming a subcommittee to "drill down further" or "refocus on the big picture," ensuring someone else does the real work.
- Propose a follow-up meeting to "balance the deep dive with broader context," buying yourself even more time.

The Backup Plan

If someone calls you out or asks for specifics, reply with confidence:

- "I just feel like there's more to uncover here, but I trust the team to decide."

- "I'm suggesting we step back because I think it'll help us clarify priorities."
- "This is more about framing the conversation—I'll defer to the group's expertise."

These responses make you seem thoughtful and collaborative, even though you've barely been paying attention.

By alternating between "drilling down" and "taking a 30,000-foot view," you've created a foolproof way to mask your lack of engagement during meetings. You're not just avoiding work—you're guiding the conversation like a true corporate Zen master. Bravo, meeting maestro!

37. Take a Sick Day by Strategically Deploying Sugar-Free Gummy Bears

Sugar-free gummy bears aren't just a sweet treat— they're your secret weapon for orchestrating a believable sick day. These notorious confections are infamous for their, shall we say, "gastrointestinal effects," making them the perfect scapegoat for an "office-wide bug" that conveniently explains your absence. With a little planning, you can set the stage for a fully credible day off, complete with delivering a karmic boomerang to any coworkers who steal snacks from you.

Step 1: Pick the Perfect Spot
Place a bag of sugar-free gummy bears in a location that screams "accidentally left behind," like:
- The corner of a shared desk.

- A shelf in the breakroom near the coffee or fridge.
- A random desk, just far enough toward the edge to suggest, "I probably meant to take this home."

Your snack-stealing coworkers will spot the unattended bag and pounce, unable to resist the lure of unclaimed gummy bear goodness.

Step 2: Pretend Not to Notice
Act as though you have no idea the gummy bears are even there. If someone mentions the bag, shrug and say, "Oh, no idea who left those". This gives the snack thieves full permission to indulge in their unearned bounty while ensuring your hands stay clean.

Step 3: Wait for the Fallout
By midday, the gastrointestinal effects of sugar-free gummy bears will start working their magic. Your target coworkers—the ones who can't resist "borrowing" snacks—will likely spend more time in the bathroom than at their desks. Keep an innocent expression as they complain about feeling unwell.

Step 4: Align Yourself with the "Bug"
Once the murmurs of an "office stomach bug" begin, casually mention that you're also feeling a bit off. Say things like:
- "Something's going around, isn't it? My stomach's been acting up too."
- "I thought it was just me, but it seems like a lot of people aren't feeling great."
- "Ugh, must be some sort of bug. Weird, right?"

This aligns your fabricated symptoms with the chaos unfolding around you, creating the perfect excuse to bow out early.

Step 5: Make Your Exit
By mid-afternoon, announce that you're heading home "just to be safe." Use phrases like:
- "I think I should rest—whatever this is, it's hitting me hard."
- "I don't want to spread anything, so I'm going to take it easy for the rest of the day."
- "Better to recover now than let this linger—I'll check in tomorrow."

No one will question your departure because the bathroom parade has already made the "bug" feel entirely plausible.

Step 6: Revel in Your Sick Day
At home, enjoy your hard-earned day off while imagining your least-favorite coworkers regretting their snack theft. If anyone checks in, respond with, "Still feeling rough, but I think I'll be okay by tomorrow. Hope everyone else is hanging in there." Sympathy guaranteed.

Advanced Techniques
For seasoned gummy-bear strategists:
- Keep a straight face if someone directly blames the gummy bears, pretending you didn't know their effects.
- Leave just enough bears in the bag to make them look like someone's leftovers, tempting the snack thieves even more.
- Suggest that maybe it's due to someone not washing the coffee mugs well enough and refer back to

number 9: Spend the First 30 Minutes of the Day Cleaning Coffee Mugs That Were Already Clean

The Backup Plan
If anyone connects the gummy bears to the office-wide misery, deflect with:
- "I never thought anyone would take them—did people help themselves to them?"

These excuses keep you innocent while highlighting the bad habits of the snack thieves.

By leaving sugar-free gummy bears in just the right spot, you've crafted a masterful plan to sabotage the office snack thieves and secure a perfectly believable sick day. Sweet revenge has never been so satisfying—or so strategically disruptive. Bravo, you gummy genius!

38. Always Have "An Important Call" When Heavy Lifting Is Required

When heavy lifting is on the horizon, there's no better escape route than an "important call." It's the ultimate excuse: vague enough to avoid scrutiny, yet crucial-sounding enough that no one will question your sudden disappearance. With a little timing and acting, you can sidestep every box, crate, and awkward piece of office furniture.

Step 1: Spot the Lifting Opportunity Early
Pay attention to any mention of physical tasks that might require manual labor, such as:

- Setting up for an event.
- Rearranging furniture in the office.
- Moving supplies, boxes, or equipment.

As soon as you hear the words "move" or "carry," mentally flag the time and prepare your exit strategy.

Step 2: Announce Your "Call"
When the time comes, casually announce, "Oh, I just remembered—I have an important call I can't miss." Use one of these scenarios to sound believable:
- "It's with a client; it could be a big deal for us."
- "It's a quick follow-up with [insert vague name or department]."
- "I have to hop on a call with IT—it's about a system issue I flagged earlier."

The trick is to sound nonchalant but slightly apologetic, as if you'd much rather be helping but *just can't get out of it*.

Step 3: Make a Quick Exit
Before anyone has time to ask questions or suggest rescheduling, grab your phone and head to a quiet corner or an empty meeting room. If you're in a shared workspace, put on your headphones and stare at your screen intently, occasionally nodding or typing as if you're deep in conversation.

Step 4: Stay "Busy" Until the Work Is Done
Remain strategically "on your call" for the duration of the heavy lifting. Occasionally pace back and forth or gesture as though you're discussing something critical. If you're in a visible area, mutter phrases like:

- "That's a great point—let me follow up on that for you."
- "Yes, I'll make sure we escalate this appropriately."
- "I completely agree; let me circle back with the team."

If anyone tries to get your attention, hold up a finger to signal, "Just one minute," while furrowing your brow to convey focus.

Step 5: Reappear Just in Time
Once the heavy lifting is done, return to the group with a look of mild exasperation. Say something like:
- "Sorry about that—important stuff, but I'm back now. Did you guys get everything sorted?"
- "That call ran a bit longer than I expected. What can I help with now?" (knowing full well there's nothing left to do).
- "Thanks for covering while I was tied up—I owe you one!"

By showing up just as the work is wrapping up, you'll appear responsible without breaking a sweat.

Advanced Techniques
For seasoned call-avoiders:
- Schedule a fake calendar event titled "Client Follow-Up" or "System Review Call" for extra credibility.
- Pretend to be "wrapping up the call" as you rejoin the group, saying, "I'll send that over shortly."
- Use this tactic sparingly to avoid suspicion—make sure it's not always *you* who's conveniently busy.

The Backup Plan

If someone questions why you're always on calls during heavy lifting, respond with:

- "It's just bad timing—I can't predict when these things come up!"
- "I hate missing out on helping, but these calls are critical to the team."
- "Trust me, I'd much rather be moving boxes than dealing with [insert vague work problem here]!"

These responses deflect suspicion while reinforcing your "busy and valuable" persona.

By always having "an important call" when heavy lifting is required, you've mastered the art of strategic avoidance. You're not just dodging work—you're prioritizing your "key responsibilities." Carry on, you clever multitasker! Or rather, let *them* carry on.

39. Pretend to Be on a Call by Dialing an Out-of-Service Number

Sometimes, you need some quiet time—and nothing is as silent as a long dead air phone call. By dialing an out-of-service number and keeping the line connected, you can log impressive talk times on your phone, giving the illusion that you're deeply engaged in a crucial conversation. It's the ultimate bluff for dodging interruptions, deflecting work, and getting that quiet break you deserve.

Step 1: Choose Your Number
Pick a number you know is out of service or will lead to a dead end, such as:

- An old disconnected number.
- The generic "test call" number for your carrier.
- Any number you know will result in silence after a brief message.

Pro tip: Test the number in advance to ensure it won't hang up on its own.

Step 2: Make the Call and Keep It Active
Dial the number and let it connect. Once the automated message plays or the silence begins, leave the line open. With most smartphones, this will count as active talk time, giving you a convincing call log as proof.

Step 3: Play the Part
While the call is live, act like you're engaged in an intense discussion. Walk around with your phone to your ear, nodding occasionally and saying vague phrases like:

- "Yes, I completely agree."
- "Let me look into that for you."
- "That's a great point—I hadn't considered that."

If you're in a shared workspace, keep your responses neutral enough that they could apply to any conversation. Add a few hand gestures for extra flair.

Step 4: Time It Perfectly
To avoid suspicion, end your "call" at a natural stopping point, such as:

- Right before lunch, so you can smoothly transition to your break.

- When a meeting starts, making it look like you were finishing something important.
- Once a tedious task has already been handled by someone else.

Hang up with a deliberate gesture and say something like, "Glad we sorted that out," or "Finally got that resolved."

Step 5: Reference Your "Call" Later
For added credibility, casually mention the "long call" in conversation:
- "That call took forever, but at least we made progress."
- "I was tied up on a call earlier—what did I miss?"
- "Sorry I couldn't help earlier; I was handling something urgent on the phone."

These statements reinforce the illusion that your call was work-related and important.

Advanced Techniques
For seasoned fake-callers:
- Use headphones or earbuds to make it less obvious that no one's talking on the other end.
- Pair your "call" with a browser tab showing a spreadsheet or report to appear doubly busy.
- Occasionally say, "I'll have to check that and get back to you," then scribble nonsense on a notepad to complete the charade.
- Throw in some personal comments like "oh yeah, how are Helen and the kids?"
- Gesture towards the phone, roll your eyes, and do a hand signal indicating that the person is a chatterbox.

The Backup Plan

If someone asks what the call was about or questions your talk time, respond with:

- "Oh, it was a client issue—just a lot of back and forth."
- "Internal discussion about something sensitive. Glad that's over!"
- "One of those never-ending calls where nothing gets resolved. You know how it is."

These vague explanations will shut down any further inquiries.

By pretending to be on a call using an out-of-service number, you've achieved peak efficiency in workplace avoidance. You're not just dodging work—you're mastering the art of looking indispensable while doing absolutely nothing. Brilliantly executed, phone virtuoso!

40. Start Your Day with a Finished Coffee Cup to Look Like an Early Bird

A finished cup of coffee on your desk first thing in the morning sends a powerful message: you've been here for hours, hard at work. This clever trick lets you skip the actual early arrival while basking in the admiration of coworkers who assume you're already on your second (or third) cup. It's a simple yet effective way to project dedication without the hassle of waking up early.

Step 1: Prepare the Evidence
Bring an empty coffee cup from home or grab a to-go cup on your way in. The key is to ensure the cup looks convincingly "used." Add some realistic details like:
- A few leftover coffee stains on the inside or lid.
- A faint aroma of coffee from an earlier pour.
- A casual splash of liquid in the bottom, as if you didn't quite finish the last sip.
- Lipstick.

Pro tip: If you're using a reusable mug, rinse it lightly but leave just enough residue to sell the illusion.

Step 2: Place the Cup Strategically
Set the empty cup on your desk in a prominent spot where your coworkers are sure to notice it. Pair it with subtle visual cues of productivity, such as:
- An open laptop displaying a spreadsheet or email inbox.
- A few scattered sticky notes with scribbled "ideas."
- A notebook with random, but official-looking, doodles.

The goal is to look like you've been working for hours and needed coffee to keep the momentum going.

Step 3: Cultivate the Image of an Early Bird
When coworkers arrive, lean into the illusion by mentioning your supposed early start:
- "I've been here for a while—already finished my first coffee!"
- "Needed a head start this morning; you know how it is."

- "I'm definitely on my second cup—these mornings are killer."

These comments reinforce the idea that you're ahead of the game while they're just getting started.

Step 4: Double Down with the Coffee Pot
If someone offers to grab coffee with you, politely decline:
- "Thanks, but I already had my fill this morning."
- "I'm trying to pace myself—I've already had a couple of cups."
- "I might grab another later, but I'm good for now."

This not only adds to the illusion but also spares you from actually having to drink more coffee.

Step 5: Maintain the Facade
Throughout the morning, occasionally glance at the cup as if fondly recalling its contents. If anyone comments on your "early start," shrug modestly and say:
- "Sometimes you just have to get ahead of the curve."
- "It's amazing how much you can get done when the office is quiet."
- "I figured I'd knock a few things out before the chaos begins."

These remarks subtly reinforce your hard-working persona without requiring any actual effort.

Advanced Techniques
For master-level early-bird impersonators:
- Pair the empty cup with a second, full cup you "just grabbed" to look even more dedicated.

- Mention something you "handled earlier this morning" to add to the illusion of productivity.
- Leave an empty coffee bag or box near your trash can to suggest you made a fresh pot before anyone else arrived.

The Backup Plan
If someone catches on and says they didn't see you come in early, respond with:
- "Oh, I was in the other room catching up on emails before settling at my desk."
- "I actually grabbed coffee at home before coming in, so I've been caffeinated for a while."
- "You must've missed me—I came in super early and then stepped out for a minute."

These explanations keep your story intact while deflecting suspicion.

By starting your day with an empty coffee cup, you've crafted the perfect illusion of an early riser and hard worker. You're not just avoiding scrutiny—you're setting the tone as a model of productivity. Cheers to your morning brilliance!

41. Invent a Mysterious Coworker Named "Steve" Who Botched Your Deliverable

When faced with missed deadlines or incomplete work, blame is the easiest way out—and who better to blame than a fictional coworker? By inventing an elusive team member named "Steve," you can shift responsibility for your botched deliverable onto a ghost employee, ensuring no one questions your competence. After all, poor Steve just can't seem to get it together.

Step 1: Introduce Steve into the Narrative
Casually drop Steve's name into conversations well before you need him as a scapegoat. Use phrases like:
- "Steve's been juggling a lot lately; I think it's affecting timelines."
- "I passed this off to Steve for review—waiting to hear back."
- "Steve mentioned he was working on this part, but I haven't seen the final version yet."

By subtly weaving Steve into your team's ecosystem, you set the stage for his inevitable failure.

Step 2: Blame Steve for the Mishap
When your deliverable falls short, pivot immediately to Steve's supposed mistakes. Examples:
- "Steve said he'd finalize this, but I guess there were some miscommunications."
- "I was relying on Steve for that piece—looks like it slipped through the cracks."
- "Steve assured me this was ready, but clearly something went wrong."

These statements deflect attention from your role while making it sound like you were misled by your (entirely fictional) colleague.

Step 3: Make Steve Unavailable for Follow-Up
If someone wants to address the issue directly with Steve, make sure he's conveniently unavailable:
- "Oh, Steve's out sick today—bad timing, I know."

- "He's on a call right now, but I'll check in with him as soon as he's free."
- "Steve's been out of the office lately; I think that's part of the problem."

By keeping Steve elusive, you ensure the blame stays squarely on his nonexistent shoulders.

Step 4: Fix Steve's "Mistakes"
To maintain the illusion of teamwork, take the high road and volunteer to clean up Steve's mess:
- "Let me fix this—I'll make sure we're back on track."
- "I'll take another look and see if I can salvage Steve's work."
- "Don't worry, I'll handle it from here."

This makes you look like a team player, even though the entire problem was your own doing.

Step 5: Retire Steve Gradually
Once Steve has served his purpose, start phasing him out of your narrative:
- "Steve's been moved to another project—he's not involved anymore."
- "Steve's workload shifted, so I'll be handling this solo moving forward."
- "Steve's focusing on different priorities now—this one's all on me."

This ensures Steve disappears before anyone starts asking too many questions about him.

Advanced Techniques
For seasoned Steve creators:
- Use a generic last name like "Smith" to make him sound more plausible: "Steve Smith in Operations."
- Add vague details to his persona, like, "He's new and still figuring out the ropes."
- Occasionally hint at Steve's quirks, like, "Steve's always so detail-focused—it slows things down sometimes."

The Backup Plan
If someone starts doubting Steve's existence, deflect with:
- "Oh, Steve's part of a different team, so you probably haven't met him."
- "Steve usually works remotely; he's not in the office much."
- "I think Steve might've been reassigned—I'll double-check."
- "Oh, there's nobody here called Steve? Damn. I've been calling that guy Steve all this time. That's embarrassing! Let me figure out his actual name and get back to you." Then don't get back to them.

These responses keep Steve's presence ambiguous while maintaining your cover.

By inventing a mysterious coworker named Steve, you've created the perfect scapegoat for any professional mishap. You're not just dodging blame—you're navigating workplace challenges with the creativity of a true mastermind. Hats off to you (and poor Steve)!

42. Keep a Stapler in Hand at All Times and Occasionally Staple Random Papers

Nothing screams "I'm busy and important" like a stapler in hand. By keeping one nearby and occasionally stapling random papers, you can project an air of industriousness without actually doing much of anything. It's the perfect low-effort strategy to convince everyone around you that you're deeply engaged in critical tasks.

Step 1: Choose Your Stapler Wisely
Invest in a professional-looking stapler. A sleek, heavy-duty model sends the message that you mean business, even if you're doing absolutely none of it. Keep it prominently displayed on your desk when not in use, as if it's your go-to tool for high-stakes paperwork.

Step 2: Always Keep the Stapler Handy
Carry the stapler with you as you move around the office. Hold it casually, as if you just stepped away from stapling something extremely important. Pair it with a stack of random papers or a clipboard for added authenticity. Optional: Clip a few spare staples to your shirt pocket for that "I'm always prepared" look.

Step 3: Staple with Purpose
Periodically staple papers together with a serious expression, even if the papers are completely unrelated. Make sure to vary your technique:
- Staple corners at odd angles, as if solving a unique organizational challenge.
- Re-staple the same papers to "correct" the alignment.

- Add an extra staple to an already-secured stack, mumbling, "Better safe than sorry."

This creates the illusion that you're constantly refining your work.

Step 4: Move Around to "Distribute" Papers

Occasionally get up and walk across the office with your stapled papers, as though delivering something important. Stop at a few desks, hand over a paper or two, and say things like:

- "Here's that update you needed."
- "Just wrapped this up—thought you'd want to see it."
- "This is good to go. Let me know if there are any issues."

Even if the recipient has no idea what you're handing them, they'll assume you're on top of things.

Step 5: Make Stapling Noises Your Soundtrack

The distinct *clunk* of a stapler is practically a productivity anthem. Use it liberally during peak office hours, but keep it subtle enough not to draw suspicion. The occasional loud staple punctuates your "work," giving coworkers auditory proof that you're "getting things done."

Advanced Techniques

For seasoned stapler strategists:

- Mix up your stapler's usage with occasional hole-punching for variety.
- Leave stacks of stapled papers around your desk to create the appearance of a backlog.
- Use colorful staples or labels to make your "work" look even more detailed and intentional.

The Backup Plan
If someone asks what you're stapling or why, respond with vague authority:
- "Just organizing some project materials—it's easier to keep track this way."
- "These are for the next meeting; I'm making sure they're ready to go."
- "You know me—always keeping things neat and tidy!"

These explanations will satisfy even the nosiest coworker while maintaining your aura of productivity.

By keeping a stapler in hand at all times and stapling randomly, you've mastered the art of looking busy with minimal effort. You're not just avoiding tasks—you're wielding office supplies like a pro. Staple on, workplace ninja!

43. Have "Wi-Fi Connectivity Issues" to Avoid Work

Few excuses are as versatile and irrefutable as "Wi-Fi connectivity issues." Whether you're in the office or working remotely, blaming unreliable internet is the perfect way to escape tasks, miss meetings, or delay deliverables. After all, who can argue with the mysterious and unpredictable forces of technology?

Step 1: Lay the Groundwork
Start by subtly hinting at your "Wi-Fi problems" before you need to use the excuse. Drop comments like:

- "My internet's been a little spotty lately—must be the weather."
- "Our router's been acting weird; I need to look into it."
- "Anyone else having connectivity issues today? Could be something with the network."

This sets the stage for a believable claim when your "issues" conveniently strike during a critical moment.

Step 2: Choose the Right Timing
Deploy the excuse at key moments to maximize its effectiveness, such as:
- Right before a meeting you don't want to attend.
- When a deadline is looming, and you haven't started the work.
- During a collaborative task where your absence won't immediately stall progress.

For added credibility, let the issue appear gradually, starting with laggy responses or occasional disconnections.

Step 3: Make the Announcement
When the time comes, report your "connectivity issues" in a way that sounds both apologetic and out of your control. Use phrases like:
- "Sorry, my Wi-Fi is acting up—I might drop off for a bit."
- "Looks like my connection's unstable. I'm working on it!"
- "I'm having internet issues on my end. Trying to troubleshoot now."

These statements deflect blame while buying you time.

Step 4: Pretend to Troubleshoot
To sell the illusion, spend time "fixing" your internet while doing whatever you actually want to do. Say things like:
- "Rebooting the router—this might take a minute."
- "I'm switching to a hotspot. Should be back up shortly."
- "Running some diagnostics now—fingers crossed!"

Bonus: Turn off your video or microphone during a meeting and claim your bandwidth can't handle it.

Step 5: Use the Excuse to Bow Out
If the Wi-Fi "issues" persist, gracefully excuse yourself:
- "I'm going to step away and sort this out—feel free to continue without me."
- "Unfortunately, my internet's not cooperating. I'll catch up later!"
- "I'll try to get reconnected, but if not, I'll follow up as soon as I can."

Your team will sympathize with your plight while you enjoy a break from responsibilities.

Advanced Techniques
For Wi-Fi excuse veterans:
- Blame specific culprits like "construction in the area" or "an outage affecting the neighborhood."
- Randomly freeze during video calls (just turn off your camera momentarily) and then "disconnect" entirely.
- Claim you're tethering to your phone and have limited data, so you need to minimize online activities.

The Backup Plan
If someone questions your Wi-Fi woes, pivot with:
- "It's usually fine—this is such bad timing!"
- "I think my provider's having issues. I'll check the outage map."
- "Technology, right? I'll get this sorted ASAP."

These responses make your excuse sound plausible while maintaining your credibility.

By claiming Wi-Fi connectivity issues, you've unlocked a foolproof way to avoid work while appearing completely blameless. You're not just dodging tasks—you're mastering the delicate art of modern workplace evasion. Stay (un)connected, genius!

44. Ask a Coworker to "Bring You Up to Speed" After Wi-Fi Issues—and Turn It into a Chat Session

Wi-Fi "issues" are the gift that keeps on giving, especially when you use them as an excuse to waste even more time chatting with coworkers. By claiming you missed key updates during your "connectivity troubles," you can justify long, meandering conversations under the guise of catching up. Bonus: You'll look proactive and engaged while contributing absolutely nothing.

Step 1: Set the Stage
Before initiating the chat, mention your earlier "Wi-Fi issues" to make your excuse airtight. Say something like:

- "I had some connection problems earlier—sorry if I missed anything important."
- "I think my Wi-Fi cut out for a bit during the meeting. What did I miss?"
- "While my connection was down, I feel like I missed some key points. Can you fill me in?"

Your coworker will likely feel obligated to help, giving you an easy entry point for a long, unproductive conversation.

Step 2: Let Them Start Explaining
Once they begin recapping what you "missed," nod thoughtfully and interject with vague affirmations:
- "Oh, that makes sense."
- "Got it—thanks for clarifying."
- "I figured it was something like that, but I wasn't sure."

This keeps the chat flowing while making it seem like you're actively listening.

Step 3: Steer the Conversation Off-Track
After they've explained the basics, pivot the discussion toward tangential or irrelevant topics. For example:
- "That reminds me—did you ever hear back about [random unrelated task]?"
- "Speaking of which, how's your [project, weekend plans, or random hobby] going?"
- "I always wonder how those decisions are made. What do you think about it?"

These diversions transform a quick catch-up into a full-blown chat session.

Step 4: Keep the Momentum Going
To extend the conversation, ask open-ended questions that invite more discussion:
- "What's your take on that decision?"
- "Do you think this will impact us long-term?"
- "How do you usually handle stuff like this? I'd love your input."

Your coworker will appreciate the attention, even though your true goal is to keep talking and avoid actual work.

Step 5: Thank Them Profusely
When the chat finally winds down (or you sense they're catching on), wrap things up with gratitude:
- "Thanks for catching me up—I really appreciate it!"
- "You're a lifesaver. This makes so much more sense now."
- "Let me know if there's anything else I should know—I owe you one!"

This makes it seem like you value their time, even though you just burned a solid chunk of it.

Advanced Techniques
For seasoned chat-wasters:
- Pretend you're still piecing things together: "Wait, so was that related to the thing we talked about last week?"
- Suggest a follow-up conversation: "We should sit down later and go over the details more thoroughly."
- Loop in a third coworker for "another perspective," further extending the discussion.

The Backup Plan

If someone questions why you're spending so much time chatting, say:

- "I just wanted to make sure I had the full picture before moving forward."
- "It's better to clarify things now than risk misinterpreting something later."
- "Collaboration is key—it's worth taking the time to align."

These excuses frame your time-wasting as diligent teamwork.

By asking a coworker to "bring you up to speed" after fake Wi-Fi issues, you've found the perfect excuse to waste time while looking engaged and responsible. It's not just a conversation—it's strategic procrastination. Brilliant move, communication connoisseur!

45. Interrupt Meetings with "Sorry, Just a Quick Question" That's Not Quick

Nothing derails a meeting quite like an unexpected "quick question" that's anything but. By interjecting with a deceptively innocent phrase, you can hijack the agenda, waste time, and make yourself seem deeply invested in the discussion—all while doing little to move it forward. It's the perfect strategy for stretching meetings without contributing anything meaningful.

Step 1: Pick Your Moment

Wait for a lull in the conversation or a natural transition point, such as:

- When someone asks, "Any questions?"
- Just as the meeting is about to move on to the next topic.
- During a lengthy explanation where it seems like no one else is fully engaged.

This ensures your interruption feels "helpful" rather than disruptive.

Step 2: Start with the Magic Words

Preface your interruption with the classic opener:

- "Sorry, just a quick question..."
- "If I could jump in for a second—quick question."
- "Before we move on, I have a quick question about that."

The word "quick" makes everyone assume your input will be brief, lowering their guard.

Step 3: Unleash Your Long-Winded Question

Once you have the floor, launch into a question that's overly broad, needlessly detailed, or tangentially related to the topic. For example:

- "Can we go back to what you mentioned earlier about [random detail] and break it down a little more?"
- "I was just wondering how this ties into [different but somewhat related project]. Could you elaborate?"
- "What's the timeline on this? And by timeline, I mean the approvals, dependencies, and follow-ups—just to clarify."

Keep layering sub-questions or follow-ups to ensure your "quick" inquiry snowballs into a time-sucking detour.

Step 4: Engage the Room
Draw others into the discussion to stretch things out even further. Use phrases like:
- "Does anyone else have thoughts on this?"
- "I'd love to hear [specific coworker]'s take on this."
- "Maybe we should brainstorm a little more around this idea."

The more people you involve, the longer the interruption will last.

Step 5: Pretend to Wrap It Up
When the facilitator starts nudging the meeting back on track, act like you're winding down but keep adding more:
- "Thanks for clarifying—one last thing, though..."
- "That makes sense, but now I'm wondering about..."
- "I think I'm getting it, but could you expand on..."

This creates the illusion that you're almost done, while sneakily extending the conversation.

Advanced Techniques
For seasoned interrupters:
- Use vague buzzwords like "synergy," "alignment," or "impact" to make your question sound more important.
- Suggest creating a separate document or action plan based on your "quick question," ensuring the detour spirals into a whole new task.
- If time runs out, say, "We can table this for later," subtly implying it should come up again in the future.

The Backup Plan

If someone gets annoyed and tries to move the meeting along, respond with:

- "I just wanted to make sure we weren't missing anything critical."
- "It seemed important to address before we moved on—thanks for indulging me."
- "Sorry for going off track; I just had a lot of thoughts on this."

These statements make you sound thoughtful and invested, even if your real goal was to waste time.

By interrupting meetings with "Sorry, just a quick question," you've mastered the art of derailing discussions while appearing engaged. You're not just asking questions—you're reshaping the agenda in your favor. Well played, meeting maestro!

46. Volunteer to Research New Software and Spend the Day Watching Tutorials

Researching new software sounds like a proactive and valuable contribution to the team, but in reality, it's the ultimate time-wasting loophole. By volunteering to take on this task, you can spend the entire day watching tutorials, clicking around menus, and pretending to assess the software's "potential," all while avoiding real work.

Bonus: you'll look tech-savvy and forward-thinking while doing it.

Step 1: Volunteer With Enthusiasm
When someone suggests exploring a new software tool or system, be the first to raise your hand:
- "I'd love to dig into this—I'm always curious about new tools."
- "Let me research this and see if it fits our needs."
- "I can take a look and put together some recommendations."

Your coworkers will be relieved they don't have to do it and impressed by your eagerness.

Step 2: Dive Into Tutorials
Start your "research" by finding tutorials for the software. YouTube, official product sites, and forums are goldmines for video walkthroughs and demos. Play them on a loop, pausing occasionally to take fake notes. Look engaged by occasionally muttering things like:
- "That's a cool feature."
- "Hmm, I didn't know it could do that."
- "Interesting—might need to explore that more."

The longer the tutorial, the better—it means less time pretending to actually use the software.

Step 3: Click Around Without a Goal
Open the software and explore its interface. Aimlessly click through menus and features while nodding thoughtfully, as if uncovering hidden gems of functionality. Occasionally say:
- "This could streamline things for us."
- "I see potential here, but it'll need some configuration."
- "This might require training, but it looks promising."

Keep your movements deliberate and slow to make it seem like you're carefully analyzing its usability.

Step 4: Avoid Drawing Conclusions
When asked about your findings, avoid giving definitive answers. Instead, focus on how "comprehensive" the software is and how much there is still to explore:
- "It's got a lot of features, but I need more time to evaluate the full scope."
- "The tutorials are great, but I'm still digging into how it might integrate with our workflows."
- "It seems powerful, but I want to make sure I'm not missing anything critical."

These vague responses will buy you more time to "research."

Step 5: Suggest a Trial Period
When pressed for recommendations, stall further by suggesting a trial run:
- "I think it'd be smart to test this with a small group to see how it performs."
- "A pilot phase would give us real-world insights we can't get from tutorials alone."
- "I'll draft a plan for how we can experiment with this before fully committing."

This ensures the task remains in limbo while you continue watching videos and tinkering.

Advanced Techniques
For seasoned software researchers:
- Watch tutorials for similar tools to "compare features." This adds hours of distraction to your day.

- Share screenshots of random software menus with comments like, "Exploring this feature now—looks promising!"
- Propose scheduling a team demo where *you* present your findings, buying yourself even more time to procrastinate.

The Backup Plan

If someone pushes for results or questions your pace, respond with:

- "I want to make sure we're thorough before recommending anything."
- "It's a complex tool—I'm prioritizing quality over speed."
- "Better to spend time upfront understanding it than waste time later if it doesn't fit."

These statements make you sound diligent and thoughtful, even though you've just spent the day passively absorbing tutorial content.

By volunteering to research new software, you've created the perfect excuse to avoid work while looking like a tech-forward hero. You're not just procrastinating—you're pioneering the future of workplace efficiency. Take a bow, software sleuth!

47. Master the Art of Strategic Sighing

A well-timed sigh is one of the most underrated tools for looking busy at work. By mastering the art of sounding overwhelmed without saying a word, you can convince your coworkers (and boss) that you're buried under a mountain of tasks—all while doing next to nothing. The key lies in timing, tone, and pairing your sighs with just the right gestures.

Step 1: Perfect Your Sigh
A convincing "busy sigh" should sound exasperated but not defeated. Practice a few variations to use in different scenarios:

- **The Quick Exhale**: A short burst of air through the nose, perfect for signaling minor frustration.
- **The Deep Sigh**: A long, audible exhale that suggests you've been working non-stop.
- **The Combo Sigh**: Pair a deep sigh with a slight groan or mutter, like "Ugh, where do I even start?" for maximum effect.

Experiment until you find your signature sound.

Step 2: Pair the Sigh with a Gesture
A sigh on its own is good, but when combined with a physical action, it becomes great. Try:

- Rubbing your temples or pinching the bridge of your nose.
- Leaning back in your chair and staring at your screen with an expression of mild despair.
- Shuffling papers or tapping furiously on your keyboard before sighing and pausing dramatically.

These gestures enhance the illusion of someone juggling a relentless workload.

Step 3: Deploy Your Sigh Strategically
Use your sighs at key moments when others are likely to notice:
- **During Meetings**: Let out a subtle sigh while reviewing documents or typing notes. If asked, say, "Just trying to keep up with everything."
- **In the Breakroom**: Sigh over your coffee while muttering, "No rest for the weary."
- **At Your Desk**: Sigh loudly enough for nearby coworkers to hear, followed by a soft, "Alright, let's tackle this…"

These moments make you seem like you're constantly on the go, even if you're doing absolutely nothing.

Step 4: Respond to Concern
If someone asks if you're okay, capitalize on their sympathy:
- "Oh, I'm fine—just a lot on my plate right now."
- "It's been non-stop, but I'll get through it."
- "Just juggling a few deadlines—it's one of those days!"

These responses reinforce the idea that you're swamped with work while subtly discouraging follow-up questions.

Step 5: Mix Up Your Repertoire
To keep your sighs believable, vary your approach throughout the day. Combine them with other vocal cues like:
- A frustrated "Huh" while shaking your head.
- A soft "Wow" as you scroll through your screen.
- A resigned chuckle followed by, "Well, here we go again."

The variety will make your "busyness" feel authentic and spontaneous.

Advanced Techniques
For seasoned sigh strategists:
- Pair your sigh with a fake call or email: "Ugh, another client request—guess I know what I'm doing for the next hour."
- Use sighs to deflect interruptions: "Can't talk right now—really trying to focus on this."
- Drop vague hints of overwork to others, like, "I'll probably be here late again."

The Backup Plan
If someone questions your workload, pivot with:
- "It's just one of those weeks—everything's hitting at once."
- "I'm trying to prioritize, but it feels like everything's urgent."
- "I think I'm managing, but it's definitely a lot right now."

These responses solidify your reputation as the office workhorse, even if you've barely lifted a finger.

By mastering the art of strategically sighing, you've created an effortless way to look perpetually busy. You're not just avoiding tasks—you're crafting an Oscar-worthy performance of workplace hustle. Bravo, sighing savant!

48. Start Conversations About Last Night's Game to Eat Up the First 10 Minutes of Meetings

Sports are the great unifier of workplace small talk—and the ultimate tool for wasting time in meetings. By bringing up last night's game (or any major sporting event), you can effortlessly derail the start of any meeting while looking like a team player who's building camaraderie. Even better, sports conversations can stretch endlessly, ensuring a productive-looking but action-free kickoff to your day.

Step 1: Choose the Game Strategically
Pick a recent game or sporting event that's likely to resonate with at least a few coworkers. This could be:
- A major playoff or championship game.
- A highly anticipated matchup between rival teams.
- Even a bizarre or controversial moment from a game you didn't watch (you don't actually need to know much—just follow the headlines).

If you don't follow sports, spend two minutes googling highlights or checking social media for key talking points.

Step 2: Open the Meeting Casually
As soon as the meeting begins, start with an enthusiastic or curious comment:
- "Did anyone catch the game last night? That ending was wild!"
- "Man, what a performance by [team/player]. Thoughts?"
- "I'm still trying to wrap my head around that call— what did you all think?"

Your coworkers will gladly jump in, especially if they're trying to avoid the agenda as much as you are.

Step 3: Let the Conversation Flow
Once the topic is introduced, step back and let the sports enthusiasts take over. Nod along, offer generic remarks like "Totally!" or "Yeah, unbelievable," and occasionally throw in a question to keep things going:

- "Do you think they'll make it to the finals?"
- "What was with that penalty in the third quarter?"
- "Is [star player] living up to the hype, or what?"

The longer they talk, the more time you've successfully wasted.

Step 4: Keep It Inclusive
If someone looks disengaged (maybe they're not into sports), loop them in by pivoting to general topics like:

- "Even if you didn't watch, you've probably heard about it by now!"
- "I swear, even non-sports fans would've loved that finish."

This ensures the entire room gets swept up in the conversation, buying you extra minutes.

Step 5: Pretend to Transition Back
After 8–10 minutes, glance at the clock and say something like:

- "Alright, we could probably talk about this all day, but I guess we should get started."
- "Great chat—let's dive into the agenda before we run out of time."

- "Thanks for indulging me on that—I needed to decompress after that game!"

This makes it look like you're the one keeping things on track, even though you orchestrated the entire delay.

Advanced Techniques
For seasoned sports-time-wasters:
- Bring up fantasy leagues or bets: "That game destroyed my fantasy points—how's everyone else doing this season?"
- Mention a future game: "Looking ahead to this weekend—any predictions?"
- Highlight controversy: "Did you see the refs trending on Twitter? Total chaos!"

These topics have endless conversational legs and can bleed into the next meeting if you're lucky.

The Backup Plan
If someone grows impatient and wants to refocus, respond with:
- "Sorry, I just got carried away—it was such a good game!"
- "Sports always bring out the passion in me. Okay, back to work!"
- "I thought a quick icebreaker might loosen everyone up before we dive in."

These responses frame your time-wasting as team-building, making you look like the glue holding the group together.

By starting conversations about last night's game, you've mastered the art of turning meetings into casual catch-up sessions. You're not just avoiding work—you're fostering "team spirit." Game on, MVP of slacking!

49. Always Have a Random Spreadsheet

Nothing says "I'm busy and important" like a spreadsheet. By keeping a random spreadsheet at the ready, you can take guilt-free breaks under the guise of crunching numbers, analyzing data, or tracking critical metrics. If anyone asks for a copy, you have the perfect excuse: *"oh no! it didn't save!"*, so now you have to spend hours "redoing" everything. This genius strategy keeps you looking productive while buying endless downtime.

Step 1: Create Your Fake Spreadsheet
Before you need it, whip up a spreadsheet that looks vaguely important but means absolutely nothing. Ideas include:
- A list of random numbers with meaningless labels like "Q3 Data" or "Cost Analysis."
- A calendar with color-coded cells and no clear purpose.
- A "to-do list" filled with generic tasks like "Update System," "Check Reports," and "Review Goals."

Make it just messy enough to appear like real work but nonsensical enough that no one will actually want to dig into it.

Step 2: Use the Spreadsheet Strategically
Whenever you feel the need for a break, open the spreadsheet and click around with purpose. Pretend to be absorbed by its contents, occasionally typing or adjusting

cells. Pair this with furrowed brows, sighs, and the occasional shake of your head to sell the illusion of deep concentration.

Pro tip: Use shortcuts like *Alt+Tab* to toggle back to the spreadsheet if someone approaches your desk unexpectedly.

Step 3: Respond Vaguely When Asked About It

If a coworker asks what you're working on, keep your explanation vague yet confident:

- "Just cleaning up some old data for [insert random project]."
- "It's a quick analysis to support a decision—nothing major."
- "I'm updating this report for alignment with next quarter's goals."

These phrases sound legitimate while ensuring no one asks for further details.

Step 4: Deflect Requests for a Copy

If someone dares to ask for a copy of your "work," act surprised and disappointed:

- "Oh no, I thought it auto-saved, but it didn't! I'll have to redo it."
- "I was almost done, and then my computer froze—everything's gone."
- "I was just prototyping—this version isn't ready to share yet."

These excuses buy you more time to keep pretending, and since there's "nothing to share," the conversation ends there.

Step 5: "Redo" the Spreadsheet Slowly

If you're pressured to recreate the spreadsheet, draw out the process by saying:

- "I need to gather the numbers again—it'll take a while."
- "I'm rechecking everything to make sure it's accurate this time."
- "I'll get to it once I finish some other priorities."

By the time you "redo" it (if ever), the person will likely have forgotten or moved on.

Advanced Techniques

For seasoned spreadsheet slackers:

- Add random formulas to make it look more complex: "=SUM(A2:A10)" or "=IF(B2>10,'Yes','No')."
- Color-code cells or create a bar chart to make it visually impressive without any actual meaning.
- Occasionally mumble things like, "Why isn't this adding up?" or "That doesn't look right."

The Backup Plan

If someone questions the authenticity of your spreadsheet, pivot with:

- "It's part of a bigger project—I'm just handling one piece of it."
- "This is more for internal use; it's not polished yet."
- "I'm testing some ideas here before finalizing the format."

These responses maintain the illusion of productivity while deflecting suspicion.

By always having a random spreadsheet at the ready, you've created the perfect shield against work interruptions. You're not just avoiding tasks—you're mastering the art of workplace theater. Excel-lent move, spreadsheet savant!

50. Tell Every Coworker, "I Think You and I Are the Only Ones Who Ever Do Any Work Around Here"

Flattery is the ultimate workplace shortcut, and nothing strokes a coworker's ego like suggesting they're part of an elite, hardworking duo—you and them. By casually dropping this line to each coworker, you not only convince them you appreciate their efforts but also subtly align yourself with their perceived work ethic. The brilliance lies in saying it to *everyone* while making each person feel uniquely valued.

Step 1: Choose Your Moment
Wait for a natural opening in conversation, like:
- After a coworker mentions a project they're working on.
- During a slow moment when others appear distracted or disengaged.
- When someone expresses frustration about workload or office dynamics.

These are prime opportunities to deliver your line with maximum impact.

Step 2: Deliver the Line with Genuine Conviction

Look your coworker in the eye, lower your voice slightly, and say:

- "You know, I feel like you and I are the only ones who actually get things done around here."
- "Honestly, if it weren't for us, I don't know what this place would do."
- "I swear, sometimes it feels like we're carrying the whole team."

The key is to sound earnest, as if you've been holding this thought for a while and just *had* to share it.

Step 3: Reinforce Their Contribution

After delivering the line, immediately follow up with a compliment specific to them:

- "I mean, look at what you just finished—it's miles ahead of what most people do."
- "I always notice how much effort you put into everything—you're one of the few I can count on."
- "Your work ethic stands out—it's refreshing, honestly."

This ensures they walk away feeling appreciated and, more importantly, like *you're* on their side.

Step 4: Watch the Magic Happen

As your coworkers start to believe they're part of an exclusive club of hardworking employees, they'll naturally start liking you more. They'll also associate you with their own perceived diligence, boosting your reputation without you having to lift a finger.

Step 5: Use It on Everyone
To maximize the impact, repeat the line with *every coworker*, tailoring it slightly for each one. Since no one will compare notes on such a flattering comment, you'll effectively convince the entire office that:
1. They're hardworking.
2. You're hardworking.
3. Everyone else is slacking off.

This combination fosters goodwill, strengthens alliances, and keeps you in the clear.

Advanced Techniques
For seasoned flattery pros:
- Add a conspiratorial tone: "It's nice to know someone else here actually gets it."
- Suggest shared frustration: "Sometimes I feel like no one else even notices how much we do."

The Backup Plan
If someone asks why you think others aren't pulling their weight, deflect with:
- "Oh, I don't mean to sound harsh—it's just a vibe I get sometimes."
- "Maybe they're busy with things we don't see, but it feels like we handle the visible stuff."
- "I'm sure they're trying, but it's just hard to match the kind of effort you and I put in."

These responses maintain the illusion without stirring office drama.

By telling every coworker, "I think you and I are the only ones who ever do any work around here," you've mastered the art of flattery as a workplace strategy. You're not just avoiding tasks—you're cultivating loyalty and admiration with a single line. Genius move, office charmer!

Closing Thoughts

Congratulations! You've reached the end of **"The Art of Doing Less at Work"**—and, if you've been following the tips within, you've probably done it during company time. Well done, slacker extraordinaire.

This book wasn't just about dodging tasks and perfecting the art of looking busy—it was about embracing the humor in workplace absurdity and reminding ourselves that, sometimes, it's okay to coast. Life's too short to spend every moment buried in reports, glued to emails, or pretending that every meeting is vital to the future of humanity.

Here's the truth: no matter how many extra hours you put in or how much of yourself you give to the job, most companies would replace you in a heartbeat if they needed to. So why sacrifice your life for their bottom line? Work hard enough to pay your bills, save for your dreams, and build the life *you* want—but never let a job become your identity or take more of you than it deserves.

Work to live, don't live to work.

Whether you're *quiet quitting,* coasting to retirement, or just having a little fun with office life, remember this: success isn't about doing everything—it's about doing just enough to get by and still make it look effortless.

So, take these strategies and use them wisely (or not-so-wisely). Share a laugh with your coworkers, enjoy the occasional "Wi-Fi outage," and never underestimate the power of a well-timed sigh.

And if anyone asks how you've suddenly become so efficient at avoiding unnecessary stress, just tell them, "I read it in a book."

Now, go forth and master the fine art of doing less. You've earned it.

The End
(Or just the beginning of your newfound freedom).

Made in the USA
Columbia, SC
05 December 2024

48546405R00085